Praise for #1 *New York Times* bestselling author
Linda Cobb
THE QUEEN OF CLEAN®!

"Linda Cobb, the self-styled Queen of Clean®, sweeps into the big time with spotless timing for a book on dirt. . . . *Talking Dirty with the Queen of Clean®*. . . has certainly cleaned up."

—*People*

"There's no stain Linda Cobb can't tame."

—*New York Post*

"She's witty, warm, a walking encyclopedia. Linda Cobb knows how to take the 'oops' out of life!"

—Carole Arnold, METRO TALK 14,
KNOR Radio, Oklahoma City

"Her enthusiasm is contagious, and her cleaning tips are both effective and fun. When Linda talks dirty everybody listens. She truly is the Queen of Clean®."

—Joe Daily, morning show host,
WBNR Radio, New York

"We all look for solutions to life's little accidents that spot our daily lives. Linda helps with simple remedies using everyday products. *Talking Dirty with the Queen of Clean®* is a must-read and a book to have at your side at all times. You're in for a real treat."

—John Nuzzo, WBVP Radio,
Beaver Falls, Pennsylvania

Talking Dirty
with the
Queen of Clean®

and

Talking
Dirty Laundry
with the
Queen of Clean®

LINDA COBB

POCKET BOOKS

New York London Toronto Sydney Singapore

An *Original* Publication of POCKET BOOKS

 POCKET BOOKS, a division of Simon & Schuster, Inc.
1230 Avenue of the Americas, New York, NY 10020

ISBN: 0-7434-4917-7

First Pocket Books trade paperback printing November 2001

10 9 8 7 6 5 4 3 2

For information regarding special discounts for bulk purchases, please contact Simon & Schuster Special Sales at 1-800-456-6798 or business@simonandschuster.com

Cover photo by John Hall
Cover design by Carolyn Lechter

Book designed by Helene Berinsky

Interior illustrations by Jeff Jones

These titles were previously published individually by Pocket Books

Printed in China

Talking Dirty
with the
Queen of Clean®

My grateful thanks to:

My husband John, The King. You put the magic in my life and the joy in my heart. You can talk dirty to me anytime!

My Mom, The Queen Mother and my best friend. Thanks for the *gift of gab,* your laughter and your gentle, loving heart.

My Dad (1905–1995). You taught me to live my life as a person, not as a girl, and you were way ahead of your time. I owe you so much, Dad. You will be in my heart forever.

My cousin Charlene. What can you say about a woman who changed your diapers when you were a baby and still loves you!

David and Janette; Victoria; Pat, Laura, John and Justin; Nancy and Drew, Nanette, David and Patrick. These children and grandchildren are the gifts that we share with each other every day. They are the reason we smile, the reason we cry, and the reason we rejoice. God bless them!

Win and Carolyn Holden. "Only those who can see the invisible, can do the impossible." You saw the invisible in me and made all things possible. Your friendship is one of our greatest gifts.

Alan Centofante. You came, you saw, you believed and you convinced others. Thank you.

My KTVK-TV, *Good Morning Arizona* family. You created a monster—thanks guys!

My Grateful Thanks

My mentor, Gloria Pitzer, whose help and encouragement started me on this great adventure.

L. Michael Moretz, my former business partner and friend, who introduced me to real dirt and taught me all he knew about cleaning and disaster restoration.

Zack, The Palace Pussycat/Research Assistant. Without his tireless efforts the chapter on pet stains and problems could not have been written. Thanks, I think . . .

Judith Curr, President and Publisher, Pocket Books; your vision for "Talking Dirty" exceeded our dreams. I just love it when people have character and talent beyond my expectations, and that's exactly what our experience with Judith and Pocket Books has been.

Brenda Copeland, started out as my editor at Pocket Books, a stranger, but was really a friend in waiting. Her ability, warmth and sense of humor made this a totally wonderful, first-class experience.

All of our friends who understood why we couldn't come out and play.

And, to all of you who have Talked Dirty with The Queen of Clean®.

Because of all of you, it is good to be Queen!

— Linda Cobb

Contents

Contents

Foreword

My mother always used to say, "Don't play in the mud!" I think if she had known the Queen of Clean, she wouldn't have stressed so much.

Linda Cobb reminds me of those two brothers in the film *City Slickers* . . . you know, the ice-cream kings. "Give us a meal," they'd say "We'll match it with the perfect ice cream flavor. Salmon? No problem: vanilla bean. Beef tenderloin? That's easy: cherry walnut."

The Queen does the same with stains! "Rust on clothes? A no-brainer! Lemon juice and sunshine. Musty books that smell? Come on, challenge me! Clay cat litter."

This woman can get the stink and the stain out of anything. The Queen even makes laundry attractive. It's hard not to love someone who finds so much joy in filth.

Parents, get ready to let your kids make mud their friend! I'm just glad Linda Cobb is mine.

—TARA HITCHCOCK, *Good Morning Arizona,* KTVK-TV 3, Phoenix

More Foreword

The third Thursday of every month is a special day on our little morning radio show. That's when the Queen of Clean invites our listeners to "talk dirty to her."

She is one of the most popular guests we've ever had. After all, have you ever met someone who uses things like Tang™, lemon juice and Massengill™ to clean? Neither have we. And that's why we love our favorite Ol' Dirt Bag, Linda Cobb.

All hail the Queen of Clean!

—BETH McDONALD AND BILL AUSTIN,
Beth and Bill in the Morning,
KEZ 99.9 FM Radio, Phoenix

1

Beating the Bathroom Blues

Over the years I have found that there is one room that generates question after question and that room is the bathroom.

Once, when I was eating in a wonderful little Chinese restaurant, the proprietor—an elderly Chinese gentleman—followed me into the ladies' room to see if I thought his bathrooms were clean. He was using the methods that I had recommended on television and was making his own cleanser from my recipe. Let me tell you, his bathrooms were spotless! It made me think that of all the rooms in your house, the bathroom is probably the room that most guests always see and have the most private time to observe. I have tried virtually every cleaning product on the market and developed many of my own "Queen's concoctions"—what follows are the best and easiest cleaning tips I can offer.

Cleaning Fiberglas™ Showers and Tubs

Heat white vinegar until it is hot, but not too hot to pour into a spray bottle and work with. Spray it on the shower and tub heavily. Wait 10-15 minutes and then moisten a scrubbing-type sponge with more of the vinegar and scrub down the shower, using additional heated vinegar as necessary. Rinse well and dry.

Removing Hard-Water Marks

Many plastic-type tubs have a dimpled slip-proof bottom that defies cleaning. I have found that using a good gel cleaner or a mild cleanser, such as the homemade types listed on page 14, and a piece of fine drywall sandpaper (looks like window screen) works the best. Cut the sandpaper into a workable size, apply the cleaner and rub. Use this only on dimples in plastic and Fiberglas™ tub and shower bottoms.

Stubborn Spot Remover for Showers

For stubborn shower spots and scum buildup, use a dry soap-filled steel wool pad on a dry shower. Do not allow water to become involved in this process, as it will cause the steel wool pad to scratch. Follow up with the vinegar process described at the beginning of this chapter.

Keeping Plastic Showers Clean

To make shower upkeep simple, apply a coat of car wax. Do not use this on the floor of the tub or shower. After showering, use a squeegee to wipe down the shower door and walls, and your shower will stay clean and you'll have fewer problems with mildew.

Cleaning Porcelain Tubs

To clean and polish a porcelain tub and remove stains, make a paste of powdered alum (available in drugstores) and water. Rub well, as if using cleanser. For stains, make a paste of powdered alum and lemon juice; apply and let dry, then moisten with more lemon juice and rub well. Rinse thoroughly.

Borax and water is also a great cleaner for porcelain. Make a paste and rub well, then rinse.

Keeping Tile and Grout Clean

You can keep ahead of grout cleaning if you use a dry typewriter eraser on dry grout to remove mildew and stains as they appear. For bigger problems, make a paste of baking soda and chlorine bleach and apply to the grout. Let dry and then rinse. Do this in a well-ventilated area, using care near carpet or fabric. Even the fumes of chlorine bleach can remove color from towels left hanging in the tub area.

Tile and Grout Cleaner

Combine 2 parts baking soda, 1 part borax and 1 part hot water, adding additional water as necessary to form a thick paste. Apply to the tile and grout and scrub with a soft brush. Rinse well.

Cleaning Soap Scum and Mildew Off of Plastic Shower Curtains

Put the shower curtain in the washing machine with one cup of white vinegar, ¼ to ½ cup of your favorite liquid laundry detergent, and several old, light-colored towels. Fill the washer with warm water and run through complete wash and rinse cycle. Remove from the washer and hang on the shower rod immediately.

Cleaning Mineral Deposits from the Shower Head

Fill a plastic sandwich bag with undiluted white vinegar. Tie this around the shower head and leave overnight. In the morning remove the bag, scrub the head with a brush and it's ready to use.

Cleaning Chrome Faucets

Use white vinegar on a cloth or sponge to remove water spots and soap scum. Dry and buff with a soft cloth. Rubbing alcohol is also a great spot remover. Apply, then dry and buff.

To shine chrome or any metal fixture in a hurry, use a used dryer fabric softener sheet on a dry fixture.

Put ½ cup of baking soda down the bathroom drain and follow with the vinegar in the plastic bag—great drain opener! Wait 30 minutes then flush with water.

Removing Hair Spray Residue

You can use this formula to remove hair spray residue from any hard surface—vanities, tile, floors, walls, etc. Mix a solution of ⅓ liquid fabric softener and ⅔ water in a spray bottle. Spray on the surface to be cleaned, and wipe. Not only does it remove hair spray, it also acts as a dust repellent and shines vanities beautifully!

Removing Bathtub Decals

Lay a sheet of aluminum foil over the decals and heat with a blow-dryer on high. Work up the edge of the decal with a dull straight-edge (credit cards work great) and keep applying the heat as you pull. If the decal is stubborn, lay down the foil as necessary and heat well and peel again. To remove the residue try petroleum jelly, denatured alcohol or nail polish remover. Test these products in a small area first before applying.

Cleaning Shower Door Tracks

Plug the drain holes in the door track with a little bit of paper towel made into a ball. Pour in undiluted white vinegar. Let this soak for 30 minutes, unplug the holes and rinse the track with a spray bottle of water and run a rag down it. This will flush the accumulated build-up out of the track.

Toilet Tips

If you have indoor plumbing, then you have to clean the toilet once in a while, whether you like it or not. Follow these tips and it will be a breeze:

Tang™ Tune-Up

To keep your toilet clean and your dog happy, put several tablespoons of Tang™ Breakfast Drink in the toilet before you leave for work or at bedtime. Let it soak, use your toilet brush to swish around under the rim, and flush. The great thing about this is you don't have to worry if the kids get into the toilet bowl cleaner.

Removing Hard-Water Rings

Shut off the water at the toilet tank and flush. Spray undiluted white vinegar around the inside of the toilet, then sprinkle borax onto the vinegar. Let soak about 30 minutes and then scrub with a piece of fine drywall sandpaper (looks like window screen—available at hardware stores and home centers). If you have an old hard-water ring you may need to repeat this several times.

Plop-Plop-Fizz-Fizz Cleaning

Drop a couple of denture-cleaning tablets into the toilet and let sit overnight. Brush under the rim with your bowl brush and flush.

② Kitchen Duty

I don't think there is a room in the house that gets messy faster than the kitchen. So let's clean up!

Appliance Magic

Many of us have white appliances in the kitchen. In order to keep them from yellowing, try this formula when you clean the exterior.

Combine:

> 8 cups of water
> ½ cup of chlorine bleach
> ½ cup baking soda
> 2 tablespoons borax

Wash white appliances thoroughly (using care around carpet or fabric), rinse well and dry.

• Rubbing alcohol makes a great cleaner for the exterior of all types of appliances. Use care around flames.

• Club soda is a wonderful polish for the exterior of appliances. It doesn't have to be fresh and have fizz; even if it has lost its carbonation it works great.

• Don't grab your everyday dishcloth to wipe down appliances; it will transfer grease and smear the finish.

Cutting Boards

Remove odors from breadboards by wetting and then rubbing with a little dry mustard. Let sit for a few minutes and then rinse. To disinfect breadboards, especially wood, keep a spray bottle with 1 quart water and 3 teaspoons of liquid chlorine bleach. Spray on, let sit at least 5 minutes, and then rinse with hot water.

Broiler Pan

For quick, easy, neat cleaning, put the broiler pan in a plastic garbage bag and lay some paper towels on it. Spray with ammonia, close bag and leave overnight. In the morning, open bag (away from face, remember the fumes), wipe with the towels that are in the bag, remove, wash broiler pan and throw out the rest of the mess.

Burned-On Casseroles

Fill the casserole or pan with hot water and throw in several used dryer fabric softener sheets. Let soak (even overnight), rinse and wash.

Automatic Coffeemakers

Depending on how often you use your coffee pot and how hard your water is, you may want to do this once a month to once every 3 months.

Fill the water reservoir with undiluted white vinegar. Place a filter in the coffee basket and turn the pot on. Allow about half of the vinegar to run through and then shut off the pot. Let it sit for about 30 minutes, then turn the coffemaker on and allow the balance of the vinegar to run through. Clean the pot out well, fill the reservoir with fresh, cold water and allow it to run through. Run the fresh water through twice.

To Clean the Glass Pot

Use lemon and salt and rub with a sponge, or use baking soda and lemon juice or water and rub with a sponge. Rinse well.

To Clean the Basket and Other Parts

For white plastic units, soak any removable parts in hot water with dishwashing liquid and about ¼ cup of chlorine bleach. Soak about 30 minutes and rinse well. This helps remove the staining and oils. For dark-colored coffeemakers, use dishwashing liquid and about ¼ cup of white vinegar in the same manner as above.

Chrome Burner Rings and Guards

Remove the burner rings from the stove. Lay a single sheet of paper toweling on each pan and moisten with ammonia. Place them in a plastic bag and close the bag. Leave for several hours or overnight. Open bag (pointed away from face, please) and remove the parts. Wash, rinse and dry.

Dishwashers

To remove that milky film from glassware and clean the inside of your dishwasher, follow this procedure:

Fill the dishwasher with your glassware (no metal, please). Use no dishwasher detergent. Put a bowl in the bottom of the dishwasher and pour in 1 cup of household bleach. Run through the wash cycle, but do not dry. Fill the bowl again with 1 cup white vinegar and let the dishwasher go through the entire cycle. Now you have the film removed from your dishes and the dishwasher clean in one easy step.

Dishwasher Odor

Sprinkle borax in the bottom of the dishwasher and leave it overnight. Using a damp sponge, use the borax to wipe down the inside of the dishwasher, door and gaskets. No need to rinse, just do the next load of dishes.

Dishwasher Rust

To remove rust from the inside of the dishwasher, fill both detergent cups with Tang™ Breakfast Drink and run through the normal cycle. If rust is bad, several treatments may be required. When doing this don't put dishes or detergent in the dishwasher.

Dishwasher Spot Stopper

To keep your dishes spot-free, use this formula. Combine the following ingredients in a container with a lid:

1 cup borax
½ cup baking soda

To use: Add 1 teaspoon of the mixture to the dishwasher along with your regular dishwasher detergent.

The Pain of Drains

This is the best nontoxic drain opener you will ever use. Pour 1 cup of salt (table salt, rock salt, any kind) and 1 cup of baking soda down the drain. Follow with a kettle of boiling water. If the problem is congealed grease, it will be gone immediately. For the very best results don't use the drain for several hours. If you need a stronger product, use 2 tablespoons of washing soda (available where laundry products are sold) dissolved in 1 quart of hot water and pour it slowly down the drain. Flush with hot water after 10 minutes.

Once-a-Month Drain Cleaner

Once a month, pour a handful of baking soda into the drain and add ½ cup of white vinegar. A small volcano will erupt. Cover the drain for several minutes and then flush with cold water after 30 minutes.

Cleaning the Disposal

Keep your garbage disposer clean and free-flowing by filling the sink with 3 inches of warm water and mixing in 1 cup of baking soda. Drain it with the disposal running.

Using the Plunger the Easy Way

Yes, there really is a special way to use a plunger to make it work more effectively. Close the overflow to the sink (usually in the front of the sink) by plugging it with an old rag. If you don't do this, the water will go down one hole and come back up the overflow. Fill the sink with 4-5 inches of water. Put the cup of the plunger over the drain and press down hard. Then pull the handle up, push down again and repeat 10 to 12 times. Adding a little petroleum jelly around the rim of the plunger gives even better suction.

Microwave Magic

To clean your microwave quickly and simply, wet a dish-cloth and place it in the center of your microwave. Turn on high and allow the cloth to sort of cook for about 30-40 sec-

onds. The steam that this creates will help loosen any hard-
ened spills and you can then use the heated cloth to wipe the
inside clean. A note of caution: Don't try to use the cloth
immediately; it will be very hot. This is a great way to disinfect your dishcloth, too.

Deodorizing the Microwave

To give your microwave a clean, fresh smell, place a bowl of
water in it and add 3 or 4 slices of fresh lemon or 2 tablespoons of lemon juice. Cook on high for 30-60 seconds.

For the very worst odors, such as burned popcorn, place
vanilla extract in a bowl and microwave for at least 30 seconds. Leave the door closed for 12 hours, remove the vanilla and wipe down the inside of the microwave.

The Smoking Oven

When something runs over in the oven and starts smoking
and smelling, grab the salt. Sprinkle on a heavy layer of salt
and continue cooking. The smoke and odor will stop imme-

diately. When done cooking, close the oven and wait overnight. The next day you will be able to lift out the spill with a pancake turner!

Cleaning the Oven

Preheat oven to 200 degrees and leave on for 15 minutes. Shut off and leave door closed. Fill a shallow glass dish with ammonia and place on the top shelf. On the lower shelf place a pan filled with 2 cups of boiling water. Close the oven door and leave the pans inside 2 hours or overnight. Remove ammonia and water; make a paste of ammonia, ½ cup baking soda and 1 cup white vinegar. Spread paste over surfaces and leave on for about 15 minutes. Scrub with a sponge and steel wool pad (if necessary), then rinse. This even works on heavily soiled ovens.

Making Your Own Cleanser

For a great non-abrasive scouring powder for disinfecting, combine:

> 4 parts baking soda
> 1 part borax
> Store in a shaker container.

For a nontoxic grease-cutting scouring powder, combine:

> 4 parts baking soda
> 1 part washing soda
> Store in a shaker container.

Cleaning and Protecting Cooktops

I receive so many questions about cleaning cooktops that I decided to devote a section just to that. Actually, glass and smooth-top ceramic surfaces are fairly easy to clean if you follow a few rules when dealing with them.

Clean the surface only when it is cool, with either dishwashing liquid, a paste of baking soda and water (3 parts baking soda to 2 parts water) or a specially formulated cooktop cleaner. Apply this with a paper towel or soft cloth. Rinse thoroughly and towel dry. Do not use a soiled dishcloth or sponge to wipe the top; it may leave a film, which can cause discoloration the next time it is heated. If this discoloration occurs, remove it with a specially formulated cooktop cleaner.

Burned-on soil can be removed with a razor-blade scraper. Avoid abrasive cleaners and pads.

If your cooktop is in really bad shape, you will have to take more drastic action before you can have cleaning ease.

You can try a product called Bon Ami®, which comes in a can, much like cleansers. This product can safely be used on mirrors, windows, windshields, etc. It has a mild pumice action. Use it very carefully with a soft, wet rag to remove heavy soiling. You can also use a mild ammonia solution along with a scrubbing-type sponge. Another product that will help remove stains and burned-on food is non-gel toothpaste, applied with a soft cloth.

Follow up these cleaning procedures by washing with dishwashing liquid and water and rinsing well. Rinsing with club soda will put a nice shine on the top surface.

I have found a wonderful product called Invisible Shield® Surface Treatment. Using this allows you to do what I call "preventive cleaning." You apply this, and in the future when you clean, spills and burned-on food bead up. It makes your stovetop surface react as if it were nonstick cookware—spills wipe off with nothing more than a damp cloth. You can safely use this on all surfaces except wood and paint—even glass! Call 800-528-3149 to find out where it is sold in your area.

QUICK TIP ....

To remove stains from nonstick cookware, boil 2 tablespoons of baking soda, ½ cup of white vinegar and 1 cup of water for 10-15 minutes. Re-season the pan with salad oil.

Refrigerator Odors and Spills

When you wipe out the refrigerator, always use a cloth or sponge moistened with white vinegar. It leaves a clean, fresh scent and helps prevent mildew.

A dab of vanilla, lemon or orange extract on a small pad of cotton will keep the refrigerator fresh-smelling without a perfume odor.

Many common refrigerator odors may be removed by placing a small tub filled with charcoal in the middle rack in the refrigerator. I use the charcoal made for fish tanks.

If you are shutting off a refrigerator, be sure to prop the door open a crack for air circulation and put a container of fresh coffee grounds inside to ward off unpleasant odors. For strong odor removal, a container or nylon stocking with coffee grounds in it works wonders.

For cleaning ease, wipe the inside of the refrigerator, including shelves, with a cloth dipped in glycerin, available in the hand cream section at the drugstore. This light coating will keep spills from sticking. Even milk or sticky substances will wipe right out.

Freezers

Try using the glycerin in freezers, too. That way spills, even though frozen, wipe right out.

Wash out the freezer with a solution of 1 gallon warm water and ¼ cup borax to clean and deodorize. Rinse and dry.

Cleaning Stainless Steel Cutlery

This is such an easy way to clean your stainless steel cutlery (forks, knives, spoons). Mix the following ingredients in the kitchen sink or any nonaluminum container:

    ¼ cup chlorine bleach
    ¼ cup Calgon Water Softener®
    1 gallon very hot water

Immerse stainless steel cutlery in the solution for 30 minutes and wash as usual. This is not for use on real silver.

To remove stubborn spots from stainless steel, use a little non-gel toothpaste or some silver polish in a separate container with a little ammonia added to it. Apply this with a soft cloth; wash, rinse and dry.

Cleaning Silver Cutlery

Wash silver cutlery as soon as possible after using. This prevents tarnish-causing stains. To clean a lot of silver cutlery quickly:

Put strips of aluminum foil in a large bowl. Place the silver cutlery on top. Cover the cutlery with boiling water and add 3 tablespoons of baking soda.

Soak for 10 minutes, rinse and dry. Use care on hollow or glued pieces. Also works on silver jewelry.

You can also make your own silver-cleaning cloths. Saturate cotton squares in a solution of:

2 parts ammonia
1 part silver polish
10 parts cold water

Let cloths drip dry and use as silver polish cloths.

Stainless Steel Sinks

So much of my mail asks about cleaning and keeping up the appearance of stainless steel sinks. One such writer suggested using the sink as an ugly planter and using nothing but paper plates and plastic silverware! Take heart—here are ways to keep them clean and actually enjoy them.

Regular cleaning

Clean with a paste of baking soda and water and rinse well. Drying the sink helps to prevent water marks and rust.

Polishing

Polish with flour. Put a tablespoon of flour in a dry sink and rub with a soft cloth. Then rinse and dry. Another polish method is club soda. Put the stopper in the sink, pour in some club soda and rub with a soft cloth. Again, dry to prevent water spots.

Removing rust and water spots

Use white vinegar on a soft cloth or sponge. It will not only erase the spots, but will also brighten the sink.

Rubbing alcohol or lighter fluid will also remove rust marks. Remember the flammability of lighter fluid and use with care.

Removing stains

Prepare a paste of 3 parts of cream of tartar to 1 part hydrogen peroxide and apply it to the stains. Allow it to dry and then wipe with a wet cloth or sponge.

To shine

Coat the sink with a few drops of baby oil. Wipe it off with paper towels. If it doesn't seem shiny enough, repeat the procedure.

Erasing hairline scratches

Using very fine steel wool, gently give the entire sink the once-over to obliterate hairline scratches. Then wash and buff with a soft cloth.

Metal Cleaners

Here are some fast, easy, homemade metal cleaners. Always test in an inconspicuous spot before using.

Brass

Use a mixture of lemon juice and salt. Wipe on until clean, then rinse and dry. Not for use on brass-plated pieces.

Copper

Use ketchup or Worcestershire sauce. Wipe on, rub until clean, rinse and buff.

Gold

On small pieces use non-gel toothpaste and a soft brush, such as a toothbrush. Rinse well. Any household ammoniated cleaner mixed 50/50 with water also works well.

Chrome

Rub with aluminum foil wrapped around your finger or hand, or wipe with a dry, used dryer fabric softener sheet.

USING YOUR MARBLES

When using your double boiler, drop several marbles in with the water. If it should start to boil dry, the marbles will rattle, alerting you to the problem before the pan is ruined.

The Queen's Best Kitchen Quick Tips

To remove food odors from plastic containers, fill with warm water and add a little dry mustard—¼ teaspoon is plenty for an average-size container. Let soak for an hour or so and then wash.

• To remove stains from plastic, put the open container in the sun. For stubborn spots, brush with a little lemon juice first.

• To chase away the odor of burned foods, boil some lemon slices or 1 tablespoon of bottled lemon juice in a saucepan for a few minutes.

• To chase away the odor of fried foods, even fish, place a small bowl of white vinegar next to the stove as you are frying.

- Clean porcelain pieces and the sink by filling the sink with warm water and adding several denture-cleaning tablets.

- Remove stains from the countertop by massaging a paste of cream of tartar and lemon juice into the stain, let it soak and then rinse.

- Clean and sanitize your sponge and dishcloth by wedging them into the dishwasher and washing them along with a load of dishes. You can also wet the sponge or dishcloth and put it in the microwave for 30 seconds.

- To remove grease from wooden cupboards, apply a very thin coat of car wax, let it dry and buff.

- Do not wash silver and stainless steel together in the dishwasher. The stainless may stain the silver.

- Remove plastic stuck to toasters with a little nail polish remover. Be sure toaster is unplugged.

- Store your steel wool pad in the freezer each time you finish with it and it will never rust. Just tuck it into a sandwich bag.

- To clean a scorched pan, fill with warm water and add several tablespoons of baking soda. Boil until the scorched parts loosen and float to the surface.

- Remove rust from baking pans by rubbing with cleanser and a cut raw potato.

- Spray a grater with nonstick cooking spray before using and cleanup will be a breeze.

• Clean the outside of a cast-iron pan with oven cleaner. Clean the inside by boiling a solution of water and a couple of tablespoons of white vinegar in it. Re-season with cooking oil and store with a piece of wax paper in it after each use. Never wash the inside of the pan with soap.

• To clean the inside of a thermos, fill with warm water and add 1 teaspoon of chlorine bleach. Let soak 30-60 minutes and rinse well.

• Preserve wooden salad bowls by wiping with a paper towel soaked in cooking oil. This prevents drying and cracking. Do not immerse in water for more than just a few seconds to clean. Always dry thoroughly.

• Remove rust from a knife or other kitchen utensil by sticking it in an onion for about an hour. Move the piece back and forth to help the onion juice do its work.

• Always put glass dishes into hot water sideways and they will never break from the expansion and contraction.

LAST THOUGHT

If you or someone in your family has asthma or allergies, you know the horror of opening cleaning products and having an attack. Try a new product from a company called Soapworks. They have a line of products created by a woman in direct response to her son's asthma attacks, which occurred every time she opened cleaning products and started to clean. The product is called At Home All-Purpose Cleaner™. It can be used undiluted for heavy jobs, such as degreasing, or diluted 100/1 for light cleaning. Totally safe, user- and earth-friendly, mildly scented and it works! Check out www.soapworks.com for information on their line of fabulous products.

3

Cleaning Products You Should Never Be Without

There are five cleaning products you should never be without, and most of them are things you already have in your home. You can purchase generous-size containers of all of them for a total of $10 and they will last for months. They can be used alone, together or in conjunction with other common household products such as salt or dishwashing liquid to help you handle most of the cleaning problems in your home. They are especially good for people with allergies and those of us who want to cut back on the chemicals in our homes.

HERE'S YOUR SHOPPING LIST ....

    White Vinegar
    Baking Soda
    Lemon Juice
    Club Soda
    Spot Shot Instant Carpet Stain Remover®

Now we'll take them in order and talk about their many uses.

White Vinegar

Use white vinegar to remove heavy soap scum and mineral deposits from showers, tubs and sinks. Warm the vinegar and put in a spray bottle. Spray on showers, tubs and sinks and let soak for 10-15 minutes. Then use a nylon scrubbing sponge to remove scum. Respray if necessary. To remove mineral deposits from around drains, close drain and pour in enough white vinegar to cover the drain area. Let soak overnight, scrub with a nylon scrubbing sponge, drain vinegar and rinse.

    To remove scum and mineral buildup from shower heads and keep them free-flowing, put undiluted white vinegar in a plastic bag. Tie around the shower head overnight. Scrub head and poke any loosened mineral deposits with a toothpick, rinse and enjoy your next shower.

To remove soap scum and mildew from plastic shower curtains and liners, fill the washing machine with warm water, 1 cup of white vinegar and your regular laundry detergent. Add the curtains, along with several old, light-colored towels. Run through complete cycle and rehang curtain immediately.

Add 2-3 tablespoons white vinegar to hot water along with your regular dishwashing liquid to cut grease on dishes and crystal.

Add ¼ cup of white vinegar to the washing machine during the final rinse to soften clothes and remove lint from dark clothes.

Apply, undiluted, to the skin with a cotton ball to deter bugs—they hate the way you taste, but the odor disappears immediately from your skin.

Neutralize pet urine odor with diluted white vinegar (25 percent vinegar to 75 percent water) sprayed on carpets. Always test in an inconspicuous spot before treating a large area.

Clean stainless steel sinks with a paste of baking soda and vinegar. Don't let the foaming scare you—it works great!

Make a window cleaner in a spray bottle with ¼ cup white vinegar added to 1 quart of water.

Make air freshener in a spray bottle with 1 teaspoon of baking soda, 1 tablespoon of white vinegar and 2 cups of water. After the foaming stops, put on lid. Shake before using.

Clean vinyl floors with ½ cup white vinegar to 1 gallon of warm water.

Keep drains free-flowing with ½ cup baking soda and ½ cup white vinegar poured down the drain on a monthly basis.

After pouring in baking soda and vinegar, cover the drain for 15 minutes (it will foam). Then flush with cold water.

Clean mirrors with a solution of half vinegar and half water. Wet a sponge, soft cloth or paper towel, wash and then buff dry. Never spray water onto a mirror. Moisture that gets into the edges and behind mirrors ruins the silvering on the mirror, resulting in dark spots.

Spray vinegar on the underarms of clothes and let soak 15-30 minutes to deodorize and minimize underarm stains.

Make an excellent toilet cleaner with 1 cup borax and 1 cup vinegar. Pour the vinegar over the stained area of the toilet, then sprinkle the borax over the vinegar. Soak for 2 hours and then brush and flush.

Baking Soda

Baking soda is a great deodorizer, cleaner and mild abrasive. Use as you would a soft-scrubbing product or cleanser in tubs and sinks.

Keep food disposals fresh and free-flowing by putting the stopper in the disposal and adding 3 inches of warm water and a handful of baking soda. Turn on the disposal and let water run out.

Remove perspiration stains and odor from clothing by applying a paste of baking soda and water and letting it soak 30 minutes prior to laundering.

Mix 1 gallon of warm water and ¼ cup of baking soda. Soak freshly washed socks in this for 30 minutes. Spin out in the washer (do not rinse out the solution), dry and you will have odor-eater socks.

Clean smudges on wallpaper with baking soda and water.

Remove crayon from hard surfaces with baking soda on a damp rag.

Use on any hard surface as a mild abrasive to remove stains.

Use as a bug killer for aphids. Use 1½ teaspoons of baking soda per pint of water and apply every 7 days.

To clean grout (any color), mix 3 cups of baking soda with 1 cup of warm water. Scrub grout with a brush and rinse.

Use baking soda on a damp cloth to polish silver.

To remove burnt food in casseroles, fill dish with hot water and add 1 tablespoon of baking soda and allow to soak.

To clean up pet vomit, sprinkle on a heavy coating of baking soda. Let it absorb moisture and dry, then scoop or vacuum up. The baking soda will neutralize acids and help prevent stains. Follow with Spot Shot Instant Carpet Stain Remover®.

Remove heel marks from hard floors with a damp cloth and baking soda.

Clean screen stain and mineral deposits off of windows by dipping a soft wet cloth in baking soda and rubbing gently. Follow by washing windows as usual.

Remove streaks and greasy film from car windshields with a thin paste of baking soda and water. Rinse well.

Put in the bottom of cat litter boxes to help eliminate odor. Put in a thin layer of baking soda and then add the litter as usual. This works with clay or clumping varieties.

Lemon Juice

Lemon juice is nature's bleach and disinfectant.

Apply to clothes, undiluted, to remove fruit-based stains. Let soak 30 minutes and then launder.

Remove rust from clothes by applying undiluted lemon juice and laying the garment in the sun. It disappears like magic.

Bleach spots off Formica™ counters by using straight or mixing in a paste with baking soda.

Clean brass and copper with lemon juice and salt. Sprinkle salt on a half-lemon and rub metal, then rinse thoroughly. If you don't have fresh lemons, you can also mix bottled lemon juice and salt.

Make a cleaner in a spray bottle with 2 cups of water, 2 tablespoons of lemon juice, ½ teaspoon of liquid dish soap, 1 tablespoon of baking soda and 1 teaspoon of borax. Shake before using to clean any hard surface.

Apply lemon juice to chrome and buff to a shine.

As a bleach alternative, use ¼ cup of lemon juice and ¼ cup of white vinegar mixed in 1 gallon of warm water and soak clothes for 15 minutes prior to washing.

Remove stains from hands with lemon juice.

Bleach wooden breadboards by applying lemon juice and letting it sit overnight. Wash and rinse in the morning.

Club Soda

Club soda is the best emergency spotter there is. Keep club soda on hand to clean up spills on carpet and clothing. Remember to react as soon as possible to a spill. If you act fast, a spot shouldn't become a stain. Club soda will remove red wine, coffee, tea, pop (yes, even red pop!), Kool-Aid™ and any other spills you can think of. Lift any solids carefully off of carpet or clothes and then pour on the club soda, blotting with an old rag until all the color from the spill is removed. Don't be afraid to really wet the carpet, it won't hurt it—carpet goes through countless dippings in water as it is made. Blot carpet easily by folding a rag and standing on it, turning the rag as it absorbs moisture and discoloration from the spill. The carbonation in the club soda brings the offending spill to the surface so that you can blot it up, and the salts in it will help prevent staining.

If you spill on your clothes in a restaurant, ask for a little club soda or seltzer and use your napkin to blot the stain until it is removed. At home you can pour the club soda directly onto the spot, flushing it out.

I have found that club soda will even work on many old stains, too. Always keep several bottles on hand.

Spot Shot Instant Carpet Stain Remover®

Every home needs a good all-purpose carpet stain remover. Skip the kinds that foam, dry and you vacuum up; they leave residue in the carpet that attracts dirt. Spot Shot Instant Carpet Stain Remover® has never failed me in years of cleaning. It effectively removes water- and oil-based stains. Use it on pet stains, lipstick, makeup, hair dye, food spills, mystery spots—even old spots. Follow the label directions and you will be amazed at how well it works. It's inexpensive and available at grocery stores, Target, Wal-Mart™ and hardware stores. Make sure you have a can on hand for emergencies. It works great in conjunction with the club soda method discussed above.

4

Rust Never Sleeps

Professional rust removers are readily available at grocery stores, home centers and hardware stores. Some of them are for use only on white clothes and others can be used on colored fabrics, too. If you are using one of these chemical products, be sure to read the directions very carefully to avoid failure. If you want to remove rust from clothes with a natural, easy method and avoid chemicals, here are two ideas.

Removing Rust from Clothes

Apply lemon juice and let the item dry in the sun, then launder as usual. This is generally safe on all washable fabrics, but if in doubt try first in an inconspicuous place. Another method is to apply cream of tartar to the rust spot, gather up the edges of the material and dip the spot into hot water. Let it sit for 5 minutes and then launder as usual.

To Remove Rust from Metal

Sprinkle scouring powder on a cork, then rub the stain. Wash and rinse as usual.

To Remove Rust from Fixtures

Rub the rust spot with salt and lemon juice until the rust disappears. Then rinse and polish.

To Remove Rust from the Toilet Bowl

There are, of course, acid bowl cleaners available from grocery stores, home centers and janitorial supply stores that will remove rust from toilets, but for an inexpensive, nontoxic way to remove rust, try this: Once a month sprinkle a layer of Tang™ Breakfast Drink or lemon Kool-Aid™ on the sides of the toilet and in the water, leave for an hour, brush and flush. Repeat if necessary. (For those of you who are wondering, citric acid oxidizes the rust.)

To Remove Rust from Stainless Steel Sinks

Rub the rust spot with lighter fluid until the rust is removed, and then follow up with liquid cleaner. Be careful when you do this not to work around an open flame, and be sure you have the area ventilated adequately.

To Remove Rust from Utensils

This is a great, easy tip—try it the next time you're making a salad! Stick the utensils, such as knives, forks, etc., into an onion. Pull back and forth on the utensil and then let it sit there so the onion juice can do its job.

To Remove Rust from Chrome

This tip works great on car chrome. Take a crumpled ball of aluminum foil and rub the rust spot until it disappears.

To Remove Rust from Countertops

This works on Formica™, plastic laminates, etc. Make a paste of cream of tartar and either lemon juice or hydrogen peroxide, apply to the rust spot and allow to sit for about 30 minutes. Scrub with nylon-type scrubbing sponge and rinse. If necessary, reapply.

5

Taming Dust Bunnies Without a Whip

Dusting is one of those thankless jobs that we all have to do. No matter how many times we do it, we still have to do it again and again. These are things that you can do to make the job easier and faster.

Home-Treated Dust Cloths

There are many dusting products on the market that you can buy, but you can easily make your own treated dust cloths for just pennies. Here's how:

Use your favorite cleaning product to make up a bucket of hot, sudsy water. Add a couple of teaspoons of turpentine. Throw in some clean, cotton dust cloths, stir so that they get saturated, and let them soak for 8 to 10 hours (I usually leave them overnight). After they have soaked, wring them out and air-dry them. As soon as they are dry they are ready to use.

Mix together two cups of hot water and one cup of lemon oil. Dip lint-less cloths into the solution. Squeeze thoroughly and air-dry. Store in a covered metal can—an old coffee can works great.

Lambswool Dusters

For dusting hard-to-reach and high areas, use a good lambswool duster. Do not use a feather duster; it simply shifts the dust around. A lambswool duster attracts dust, is easily washed and can be used for years. Look for these at janitorial supply stores, home centers, in mail-order catalogs and websites that sell cleaning supplies.

Dust Repellent

To keep dust off blinds, refrigerators and glass-top tables, mix a solution of 1 part liquid fabric softener to 4 parts water. Spray on or apply with a soft cloth and dry with a soft cloth. This will repel the dust.

Dusting Prints

Use cornstarch to remove extra furniture polish and wipe off fingerprints on wood furniture. Shake a little on the surface and polish with a soft cloth.

6

Floor Cleaning—
Now Step on It

Once you know a few basics you can clean your floors quickly and easily—just like the pros.

Sealing Ceramic Tile

Sealing your grout is a must. Purchase sealer from the store where you bought your tile or from a home center.

Cleaning Ceramic Tile

Ceramic tile is not porous—you can clean effectively with warm water. Many cleaners leave a residue on the tile surface that looks like a smeary coating. A good neutral cleaner for tile is 1 gallon warm water, 2 tablespoons of ammonia and 1 tablespoon of borax. Never use vinegar. It is acidic and will eventually etch the grout.

Never use a sponge mop on ceramic tile. It works like a squeegee, depositing the dirty water into the grout tracks.

Sweep or vacuum floor prior to washing.

Use a rag or chamois-type mop.

Rinse mop, frequently changing the water as it becomes soiled.

If you have a gloss-finish tile it may be necessary to dry the tile. Use a clean terry rag under your foot to do it the easy way.

Dusting Wood Floors

Use a dry dust mop to remove dust or vacuum floor, being sure not to use a vacuum with a beater bar—this can mar the floor.

Cleaning Wood Floors with Tea

Tea is a wonderful cleaner for wood because of the tannic acid. Brew 1 quart of boiling water with 1 or 2 tea bags. Let it come to room temperature. Wring out a soft cloth to just damp and wash floor, keeping the rag clean. Do not over-wet floor. This will clean the floor and cover many imperfections. Buff with a soft cloth if desired.

Repair Scratches in Wood Floors

To fill scratches, use a crayon or combine several to match the floor. Wax crayons for wood are available at the hardware store. Work the crayon into the scratch, then heat the repair with a blow-dryer and buff with a rag. This will work the repair into the floor so well, you'll never know it's there.

Clean and Wax

There is a product made by Bruce Floor Care Products that is a cleaner and wax in one. It comes in two colors, light and dark. If your floors are very bad you might consider trying this product before you spend the money to refinish the floors. Follow the directions on the can carefully, and allow plenty of time to do the job, working in one small area at a time.

Cleaning Vinyl Floors

For cleaning vinyl floors, including no-wax floors, sheet vinyl and linoleum:

Sweep or vacuum the floor well. Mix 1 gallon of warm water and 1 tablespoon of borax. Wring out mop or rag well in the solution and wash the floor, keeping the rag clean. No rinsing is necessary. Using borax preserves the shine on floors, even those that have been waxed.

Waxing Floors

When you wax a floor it is wise to buy the wax from a janitorial store, which sells commercial products that hold up well to wear and traffic.

On a clean floor apply 2 thin coats of wax, allowing ample drying time between coats. It is imperative that the floor be clean, otherwise you will wax in the dirt.

The next time you wax, wax only the traffic area where the wax is worn off, feathering it into the other areas to blend. This eliminates wax buildup around the edges of the room.

Purchase a wax-stripping product from your local janitorial supply store. It is more efficient than ammonia and also very reasonably priced.

The Miracle of Microfiber . . . or Is It?

Microfiber cloths and mops clean without chemicals—just water and the cloth or mop. Do these products work? Well . . . yes and no. The old adage *you get what you pay for* certainly holds true in the microfiber business. If you are purchasing these cloths dirt cheap you are wasting your money. If they do not contain thousands of fibers, they won't clean as they should. Here's the dirty lowdown on the very best.

Euronet USA makes the Act Natural Mop™. A dry mop/wet mop with a telescoping handle, this miracle cleans vinyl, ceramic, wood—any hard flooring—beautifully with nothing but water. Just wring the mop out in water, stick it to the velcro pad and go! Machine wash. Check out www.euronetusa.com or call 888-638-2882.

7
Today's Wood— Tomorrow's Heirlooms

Wood furniture in a home is a big investment. Properly cared for, it will last and keep its new appearance for years, eventually to be called "antique" by our grandchildren and great grandchildren. Here are some tips to keep your furniture looking great, some tips on fixing problems that arise, plus the recipe for making your own furniture polish.

Making Your Own Furniture Polish

There are several great furniture polishes you can make at home with ease. The general rule for homemade polish is to rub it in with a soft cloth and wipe it off and buff with another clean, soft cloth.

Combine ¼ cup white vinegar and 1 cup olive oil in a clean container. Shake before each use.

Combine 1 cup of mineral oil and 3 drops of lemon extract. Shake before each use.

Grate 2 ounces of beeswax (available at drugstores) into a jar and cover it with 5 ounces of natural turpentine. Shake occasionally until dissolved, or stand in a bowl of hot water. Apply to furniture with a soft cloth (just a small amount is all that is needed) and buff with a clean, soft cloth. If it becomes hard over a period of time, set it in a bowl of hot water. This formula seems to work especially well on unvarnished furniture.

Water Marks/Heat Scars and White Rings

Massage mayonnaise into the marks and leave it on overnight. The next morning, wipe off the mayonnaise and the marks should be gone. You can also use petroleum jelly, butter or margarine. If you have a really stubborn spot, mix cigarette ashes or rottenstone (available at the hardware store) with the mayonnaise and repeat the above procedure.

Non-gel white toothpaste is also effective in removing white water rings. Dab toothpaste on a damp cloth and gently massage the ring in a circular motion until it's gone. Wipe and buff with a soft cloth. Apply furniture polish if necessary.

Remove Old Polish and Dirt

Put 2 tea bags in a pot with 1 quart of water and bring it to a boil. Cool to room temperature. Dip a soft cloth in the solution, wring it until it is just damp and wipe furniture with it. Buff it dry with a soft cloth, then decide if it requires polish.

Restoring Dried-Out Furniture

Dab petroleum jelly on a soft cloth and polish to help feed and restore dry wood. You will be amazed to see the wood grain and natural luster appear.

Cleaning Very Dirty Wood Furniture

Mix a solution of 1 quart warm water and 3 or 4 drops of dishwashing liquid. Wash the furniture with a soft cloth wrung out until it is damp, rinse and buff dry.

Covering Scratches

To cover scratches on wood furniture, use a crayon the color of the wood. Apply to the scratched area, heat with a blow-dryer and buff the crayon into the scratch with a soft cloth.

For darker woods, rub the meat of a pecan or walnut into the scratch and buff well.

To cover scratches on mahogany or cherry wood, use iodine.

Removing Stickers from Wood

To remove a price tag, identifying label or decal from wood, pull up as much of the sticker as possible, then dip a cloth in vegetable oil or baby oil and gently scrub the area until the sticker and adhesive are gone. Finish by buffing well with a soft cloth.

Off the Walls— Wash Them Like the Pros

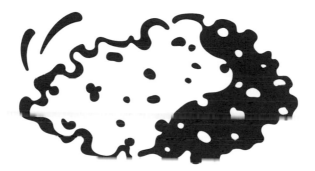

Wall-washing can actually be easy if you have the right equipment and do it the right way. Here are some tips for spotting, removing marks and washing walls.

Have All the Right Stuff

When you are ready to wash walls, be sure you gather up the right things to do the job quickly and easily. Get things together before you start and have the furniture moved away from the walls so that the washing process will flow smoothly. Do it like a professional. Here is a list of the things you should have:

> 2 buckets
> Natural sponge (not one of those awful nylon ones)
> Baking soda and a soft rag
> Art gum eraser
> Dropcloths
> Ladder
> Ingredients for cleaning solution of your choice
> 2 strips of washcloth or terry rags and 2 rubber bands

QUICK TIP

Use a dropcloth on the floor around the area you will be washing—it will save you time and mess in the long run. A fabric dropcloth is preferable to plastic, as it absorbs and isn't slippery when wet. Before you start to wash, wrap a strip of washcloth or turkish toweling around your wrist several times and secure with rubber bands. This will keep drips from running up your arms when you are working with your arms above your head.

Removing Marks

The first thing you want to try to do is erase the marks on the wall away. Use an art gum eraser that you keep on hand for this purpose and erase just the mark. This works on many types of marks. If you still have some stubborn spots, use a little baking soda on the corner of a white rag and rub gently, doing just the mark. Non-gel toothpaste also is a good spot remover; use it on a cloth over the tip of your finger.

Crayon Marks

If you have kids, you have probably had crayon on the wall. To remove crayon easily, spray with WD-40™ lubricant and wipe crayon away with a paper towel. Follow up with a soft cloth and a solution of hot water and a little dishwashing liquid, washing in a circular motion.

Ink and Marker Marks

To remove ink or Magic Marker®, use hair spray (the cheaper the better), rubbing alcohol, or for really tough spots, denatured alcohol from the hardware store. Always spot carefully, trying to do just the spot.

Great Wall-Washing Solutions

Try one of these wall-washing solutions:

• 1 gallon warm water, ½ cup ammonia, ¼ cup white vinegar and ¼ cup washing soda

• 1 gallon warm water, 1 cup ammonia and 1 teaspoon mild dishwashing liquid

For really professional results, rinse the walls with clear water after washing with either of these solutions. If you choose not to rinse, then be sure to change the cleaning solution frequently as it becomes soiled.

Where to Start

You have the wall free of marks, your dropcloths are in place, your wrists are wrapped for drips and you have your washing solution ready. Now wet your natural sponge (available at janitorial supply stores, home centers and hardware stores). Don't skimp and use a nylon sponge or a rag; it will drag as you wash and take you twice as long. A natural sponge has thousands of "scrubbing fingers" and will get the job done fast, easy and right. Begin washing at the bottom of the wall and work up, doing the ceiling last. Drips of water are much easier to wipe off of a clean wall and won't leave marks like they do on a soiled wall.

Don't Stop!

Once you start on a wall, don't stop in the middle. Complete one full wall or the full ceiling before you take a break. If you stop in the middle of a wall or ceiling you will have "tide marks" where you stop and start again.

Keeping Walls Clean

You can make your own brushing tool to use between washing, to dust down the walls. Tie a clean dust cloth loosely around a broom head and use to dust ceiling thoroughly from time to time and to dust down walls. Give the broom a shake now and then as you are working to remove dust.

Grease Spots on Wallpaper

Make a paste of cornstarch and water and apply to the grease spot. Allow it to dry, then brush or vacuum it off.

Apply a double fold of brown paper (a grocery bag works well, but don't use the part with the writing on it) and press over the grease spot with a warm iron. This may require several efforts. This method also works well on candle wax. Follow up with a little hair spray or alcohol.

Removing Crayon from Wallpaper

Rub lightly with a dry soap-filled steel wool pad. Do this very gently. You can also try rubbing with baking soda on a damp cloth. On vinyl paper, try using a little silver polish.

Smudges, Marks and Mystery Stains on Wallpaper

Erase with an art gum eraser.

To remove marks from nonwashable paper: Rub a scrunched-up piece of white bread over the marks. Rub very gently. You may need to repeat this a few times before you make progress.

Washing Wallpaper

Wash vinyl and washable papers with one of the mild wall-washing solutions in this chapter.

Cloth Wall Coverings

To clean grasscloth, burlap or cloth wall covering, vacuum with the soft duster brush on the vacuum. Do this regularly to maintain the appearance.

Wood Paneling

Clean wood paneling following the suggestions in the chapter on wood floor cleaning.

Up, Up and Away—
Upholstery Cleaning
Made Easy

This chapter will give you all the information you need to choose upholstered furniture wisely, spot-clean it, handle emergency spills and clean it thoroughly.

One of the first things everyone should know about upholstery is that there are different cleaning methods for different types of fabric. There is a simple way to check to see how the furniture you have now should be cleaned, and even more importantly, how a new piece should be cleaned. This will help you make good decisions on wearability and cleanability before you get the piece home.

Cleaning Codes and What They Mean

Upholstery is supposed to be marked with a code that allows the consumer to know in advance what type of cleaning the manufacturer recommends for that particular piece of furniture. These instructions, known as cleaning codes, are generally found under the seat cushions on the platform of the furniture (the part that the cushions sit on). I will discuss each cleaning code individually below. If you do not find the code under the seat cushions, check all tags for instructions and never buy any upholstered furniture without knowing how it can be cleaned. This information is essential.

W

If you find a W on your furniture, it means that it can be cleaned with water. This would mean that you could rent an extraction carpet and upholstery cleaning machine from the home center or hardware store or use one that you have purchased to clean the fabric. You can also use water in spotting spills. This is the most durable and cleanable fabric you can buy. It is ideal for dining chairs, family room furniture, anything that gets heavy use or where spills might occur frequently.

S

If you find an S on your furniture, it means that it must be cleaned with cleaning solvents (dry-clean only) and you cannot apply water to it. This would eliminate spot-cleaning with water-based products. Dry-clean only fabrics are generally not as durable and also do not clean as well. If you have a piece with this code, do not allow it to become heavily soiled before calling in a professional cleaner or you will be disappointed with the results. If you need to spot-clean a dry-clean only fabric, try using Energine Cleaning Fluid®, available at grocery and hardware stores. Test it first in an inconspicuous spot to be sure it doesn't damage the fabric. Apply with a clean, light-colored cloth and blot continuously. Once you have removed the spot, use a blow-dryer to dry the spot quickly so it doesn't leave a noticeable ring on the fabric.

S/W

This code means a combination of solvents and water can be used to clean the upholstery. It does not appear on many pieces. It is best left to the professionals to clean this. Use furniture with this code in low-use areas.

X

This code does not appear on furniture as much any more, but it does appear frequently on fabric blinds and shades. It means that the item is not cleanable and is a vacuum-only piece. Beware!

Don't Undress Your Furniture

Many people have asked me about taking the covers off the foam cushions and washing them in the washing machine—DON'T DO IT! The zippers are in the backs of cushions only so that the foam cushions may be changed by a professional if necessary. If you remove the cushion covers and wash them they may shrink and not fit back on the foam correctly; no matter what, it is virtually impossible to get them back on the foam forms evenly and correctly. Plus, they will be noticeably cleaner than the rest of the sofa and will fade and wear out more quickly.

Spot Cleaning

If you need to spot-clean a cushion, unzip the zipper and put a pad of paper towels or a folded white rag between the foam and the cushion covering. Apply your spotter, carefully following the directions. Try not to rub the area, as it causes abrasion on the fabric surface—BLOT - BLOT - BLOT. I have had great success with Spot Shot Upholstery Stain Remover®. It is easy to use and works on a wide variety of spills and soiling. It can be used on a wide variety of fabrics (always test any spotter in an inconspicuous area before using) and works well on the sofa or chair body as well as the cushions. It is great for food spills on dining chairs. Remember, whatever spotting method you choose, always first do a test area where it won't show.

Candle Wax Meets Upholstery

If you have the unfortunate accident of having candle wax come in contact with your upholstery, don't despair. First, put a large quantity of ice in a plastic bag and lay it on the wax long enough to allow the wax to freeze. Remove the ice and immediately chip up any wax that you can.

Next, take a brown grocery bag and, using only the part without writing, lay it over the wax. Using a medium/hot iron, press over the wax, allowing it to absorb into the paper bag. Move the bag continuously to a clean area. Once you have absorbed as much of the wax as possible, use Energine Cleaning Fluid® to spot-clean the area, remembering to use a blow-dryer to dry the spot when you are done.

If any staining remains, use 3 percent hydrogen peroxide from the drugstore applied with a spoon to bleach out the wax color. Apply peroxide, wait 15 minutes and blot, continuing until the color from the wax is gone.

10

Leather Report

Many of us have leather furniture, car interiors, clothes and accessories. Unfortunately, along with wearing leather and using it in our homes comes the frustration of cleaning it.

Cleaning Leather Furniture

Keep leather furniture out of direct sunlight, otherwise it may crack and dry out. You should use hide food once or twice a year to ensure that the leather remains supple. Make sure you rub it in well so that it does not come off on clothes. I like to apply it, rub it in well, let it sit for 12 hours and then buff again before using the piece. Dust or vacuum regularly and clean with saddle soap or wipe with a damp cloth rubbed across a wet bar of glycerin soap or moisturizing facial soap, such as Dove. If the leather piece is tufted and has buttons and piping, use a soft, bristled toothbrush or paintbrush moistened and rubbed across the soap. Always dry leather with a clean, lint-free cloth.

If you have a sealed leather table or desktop, clean, polish and seal it with paste wax once or twice a year.

Leather Apparel

If you have dirty leather shoes, purses, coats or accessories, you can treat them much the same way that you do your furniture. For cleaning purses and shoes, a damp, soft cloth rubbed across a bar of moisturizing facial soap, such as Dove, works well. You should always use care to not overwet the article. Do not rinse after washing; instead, allow to dry naturally, then polish as usual.

Water Spots

Simply run a damp sponge over the area and allow to dry.

Salt Stains

Dab on a solution of 3 parts white vinegar to 1 part water.

Ink Stains and Spots

To remove ink stains and spots from leather, apply a little cuticle remover. Dab it on the spot and rub gently with a soft cloth, wipe and buff. You may need to allow the cuticle remover to sit for 10 minutes or so before rubbing for difficult stains. Reapply if necessary.

Dark Stains

If you have light-colored leather furniture and apparel with dark stains on it, try wiping gently with a thin paste of lemon juice and cream of tartar. Gently massage in, then finish off with a soft damp cloth. Be sure to rinse well and follow up with one of the cleaning methods above.

Removing Mildew

To remove mildew from leather, apply a coat of petroleum jelly, allow to sit for 4-5 hours and then rub off.

Making Hide Food

Make your own "hide food" by mixing 1 part vinegar to 2 parts linseed oil in a jar with a lid. Shake well and apply with a soft cloth, changing it frequently as it soils. Buff well so oil won't transfer to clothes. Test in an inconspicuous area before using on light-colored leather.

11

Meticulous Marble—
Leave No
Stone Unturned

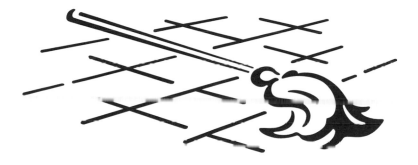

While bathroom and kitchen countertops are usually synthetic (cultured marble), marble used in living room and other furniture is usually the genuine article. Seal it with a stone sealer because it is very susceptible to stains, and wipe up spills quickly.

Maintaining Marble

Dust and/or wipe with a damp cloth as needed. Caked-on spots can be sprinkled with borax or baking powder and rubbed with a damp sponge or cloth. You can also use a commercial marble polish.

Bathroom or kitchen marble can be cleaned with ⅓ liquid fabric softener to ⅔ water. Clean thoroughly and polish with a soft cloth.

Fine Scratches

Use extra-fine steel wool to apply baking soda and water mixed to a paste. Flush with water and let it dry; repeat if necessary. Buff with a dry cloth or use a buffing wheel on your electric drill.

Grease Stains

These are circular and often dark in the center. Wash surface with ammonia, rinse with plenty of water, then repeat—OR, cover area with a ½-inch-thick paste of 20 percent hydrogen peroxide and powdered whiting from the paint store. Keep it damp by covering it with plastic wrap sealed with masking tape. After 10-15 minutes, rinse with water, avoiding any wood trim. Repeat if necessary. Buff and then polish.

Rust

Rub with a rough cloth or make a mix of commercial liquid rust remover and whiting and follow the directions for grease stains. After removing the paste, rub marble with dry cloth.

Tea, Coffee, Ink

Use hydrogen peroxide/whiting method—see grease stains method.

Water

Use hydrogen peroxide, applied with a medicine dropper, followed with a drop or two of household ammonia. After 20 minutes, wash area.

Wine

Use hydrogen peroxide.

Mystery Stains

To remove stains of an unknown origin, try hydrogen peroxide mixed with cream of tartar or non-gel toothpaste, rubbed in with a soft cloth and rinsed off.

Restoring the Polish

To restore the polish to marble, rub with a cloth dampened with turpentine.

Warm Up That Spot

Warming marble with a blow-dryer or setting the object in the sun will make the stain removal work more quickly.

12

The Queen's Royal Carpet Treatment

Carpet is one of the most expensive investments you will make in your home. With proper knowledge about choosing a good-quality carpet that fits your lifestyle, and cleaning and stain removal guidelines, your carpet will give you many years of enjoyment and quality wear.

Know Your Carpet

Most residential carpet is made from one of four fibers: nylon, polyester, olefin or wool (or a combination). All of these fibers can make great carpet, although nylon is one of the most cost-effective and durable. Here are some other things to be aware of when making that important purchase.

Face Weight is a common-sense measurement that you should be aware of when purchasing carpet. The key to remember: More fibers are almost always better.

Fiber Density is a measurement of how closely packed carpet fibers are to each other. Carpets with high density tend to look better longer and will give carpet a soft feeling when walked upon.

Carpet Fiber Twist is very important to be aware of, especially with cut pile types of carpet. Fibers that have more twists per linear inch usually make more durable carpeting.

Carpet Padding is absolutely critical to good carpet performance. Too much or too little can cause premature failure in many carpets. The best pads, believe it or not, are those that are thin and firm. Avoid pads thicker than 7/16 inch.

Cleaning Carpet

Many people ask me how to go about hiring a firm to clean carpeting. Listed below are some general guidelines to follow. Always call more than one company, looking for comparable pricing. Ask each company the same set of questions, and remember word-of-mouth is one of your best allies. Ask your neighbors, your friends, the people you work with which companies they have used and how satisfied they were.

QUESTIONS TO ASK

Cost Per Square Foot or Room

Find out if there is a square footage limitation per room and if your room sizes fit within the limitation. Remember to ask about hallways, walk-in closets and bathrooms. They may count as a whole room when companies offer room pricing. If the cost is figured by square foot, measure the length and width of your rooms and multiply length by width to achieve the square footage. Add the total square footage of all of your rooms and multiply by the cost per square foot. This should give you an accurate price.

Find Out What Method of Cleaning Is Used

Steam cleaning or extraction is the preferable way to clean. Ask if the company uses a "truck mounted unit." A portable cleaner will not generate the same powerful extraction process that a truck unit will.

Do They Clean with Hot or Cold Water?

Cold water will not remove stubborn, greasy soil. A truck-mounted cleaning system should hook up to your cold water, usually at an outside tap, and heat the water as it flows through the truck.

Is the Company Insured?

If they damage your furniture while moving it or bang

into a wall, you want to be sure they can cover the cost of the repair.

Ask About Experience
Be sure you are hiring trained professionals who do this for a living.

Remember the Investment
Again, carpet is one of your most expensive investments, so treat it with the care it deserves and it will last much longer and look better.

Before Cleaning Carpets

- Pick up all small items from carpets.

- Remove all items from furniture to be moved.

- When possible, remove dining chairs and other small, light pieces of furniture.

- Pick up all small area rugs.

- Remove things from the floor of the closet if it will be cleaned.

- Remove anything from under beds if they are to be moved.

- Open as many windows as possible, if weather permits.

- If house is not left open, turn on the air conditioner or heat, whichever is appropriate.

- If possible, set fans so they blow across the carpet.

• Wash the soles of the shoes or slippers that you will be wearing on the damp carpet, otherwise dirt from the soles will be transferred to the carpet.

• Do not move furniture back until carpet is completely dry.

After Carpets Are Cleaned

BEWARE of slippery linoleum and other hard floors when stepping from damp carpet.

• Do not put towels or sheets or newspapers on the carpet.

• If you have had the carpet treated with carpet protector, you will need to allow extra drying time.

• Vacuum carpet thoroughly after it is dry with a clean vacuum.

Spotting Guide

The number one rule of spot removal on carpet is to always keep several bottles of club soda on hand to use on spills on any kind of carpet. If you spill, follow this advice:

Blot up as much moisture as you can—laying old towels over the spill and standing on them is a great way to start.

• Scrape up any solids.

• Pour club soda on the spill. Don't be afraid to really pour it on. The carbonation in the soda will "bubble up" the spill so that you can blot it up. Again, cover the spot with clean, light-colored towels or rags and stand on them. This will really help to absorb the spill. Continue to pour and absorb until all color from the stain has been blotted up and the towel is coming up clean.

• Follow up with a good carpet stain remover. I prefer Spot Shot Instant Carpet Stain Remover®.

• When you spot-clean carpet, never rub, as it will only spread the stain and will cause abrasion to the carpet fibers.

• This is a good general cleaning method for most spills and definitely will not cause any damage.

Red Pop, Kool-Aid™

Grab the club soda fast and follow the above method. If the stain is old, still try the club soda—it will help lighten the stain. After using your carpet spotter, if the spot is still present, saturate with hydrogen peroxide or undiluted lemon juice. Wait 15 minutes and blot. Continue to apply and check your progress, just to be sure you aren't lightening the carpet.

Red Wine

Grab the white wine and pour it on or saturate with salt and follow with the club soda and carpet spotter.

Nail Polish

Blot up as much polish as possible with a tissue or anything handy. Then test the effect of nonoily nail polish remover on an inconspicuous part of the carpet. If there are no ill effects to the carpet pile, apply the nail polish remover with an eye dropper or a nonsilver spoon, blotting immediately after each application. Always use nonoily polish remover. If regular nail polish remover does not work, buy straight acetone at a beauty supply house, pretest again, and apply as directed above. Once you have removed as much as possible (have patience) follow with Spot Shot Carpet Stain Remover®, applied according to the directions. If color staining remains, apply hydrogen peroxide to bleach or lighten the stain.

Mud

Cover wet mud with salt or baking soda and let dry thoroughly before touching. Once it is dry, vacuum it using the attachment hose to concentrate the suction on the mud. Use a good carpet spotter, following the directions, to complete the process. For red dirt or mud, use a rust remover such as Whink® or Rust Magic® to remove any color residue. Make sure you test the rust remover in a small area first.

Coffee and Tea

The best defense is a good offense when you spill coffee. First, act as quickly as possible. Hot coffee is the equivalent of brown dye. Blot up all of the spill that you can and immediately apply club soda. If you don't have club soda (shame on you), use plain cold water. Really pour it on and blot, blot, blot. Follow with a good-quality carpet spotter. If a stain remains you can attempt to remove it by pouring on hydrogen peroxide, waiting 15 minutes and then blotting. If it is lightening the stain, continue and as a final step rinse with cold water or club soda.

Use Shaving Cream

The great instant spot remover! If you have a spill and have no carpet spotter available, grab the shaving cream. It is particularly effective on makeup, lipstick, coffee and tea. Work it into the spot well and rinse with either cold water or club soda.

Guide to Special Spots

Spots Such as Tar and Mustard

Work glycerin (available at drugstores in the hand cream section) into the spot. Let it sit 30-60 minutes. Working carefully with paper towels, use a lifting motion to remove the spot. This may require multiple treatments. Follow with a good spotter, such as Spot Shot®.

Removing Indentations in Carpet

Lay ice cubes in the indentations caused by furniture. Be sure to cover all of the indented area. Leave overnight and then fluff the nap with the tines of a fork the next day.

Candle Wax

Put ice in a plastic bag and lay over the wax, allowing it to freeze. Chip off all wax that you can. Next, lay brown paper over the wax (a grocery bag works great; use the area without the writing) and press with a medium/hot iron. Move the paper as it absorbs so that you don't redeposit the wax on the carpet. Have patience and continue as long as any wax shows up on the bag. Next, apply a good carpet stain remover.

Soot

Sprinkle with salt and wait at least 2 hours and then vacuum, using the attachment hose to concentrate the suction. Spot with a good spotter or Energine Cleaning Fluid®.

Gum

Freeze with ice in a bag and chip off all that you can. Work a little petroleum jelly into the remaining residue and roll the gum into it. Scrape up and follow with a good spotter or Energine Cleaning Fluid®.

Glue

Try saturating glue with undiluted white vinegar. Working with an upward motion, work it out of the fibers and spot with Energine Cleaning Fluid®. For rubber cement, use the method above for gum.

Ink

Spray on hair spray or blot with rubbing alcohol. For heavy spots, try denatured alcohol. Blot well and follow with a spotter.

Armed for Battle

Always keep a good carpet spotting product on hand! I have found an incredible product that removes not only fresh red stains, but also old ones. It will work effectively on such things as red wine, red pop, Kool-Aid™, cranberry juice, red food coloring and even black coffee and tea. It is called Wine Away Red Wine Stain Remover™. Don't let the name fool you, if you are a mom you need this product, if you drink red wine you need it too! It is totally nontoxic and works on carpet and upholstery, even car seats. Call 888-WINEAWAY for a purchase location near you.

13

Are Pets Turning Your Home into a Barnyard?

Do your pets have accidents in the house? Did you have a pet-sitter while you were on a trip and the cat didn't use the litterbox and the dog didn't go outside? Do you know what to do when the cat leaves you a hairball surprise on the carpet or the spaghetti didn't agree with the dog? Help is on the way! Here's all the information you need to clean up pet accidents and keep them from happening again.

Pet Odor

Pet odor caused from urine or feces is one of the toughest deodorizing problems you will face. The stain from the problem is only a small part of the dilemma. Unless you completely deodorize the area where the pet accident occurred, the animal, especially cats, will return to the spot and resoil it.

Pet odor is a protein-based problem and cannot be eliminated by normal spotting procedures. In order to remove odor, you must use an enzyme product to digest the protein, particularly in urine. If you do not use the correct cleaning procedure, the cat or dog will locate the smell and re-use the area, since animals operate primarily on a sense of smell.

Enzyme products may be purchased at pet supply stores, veterinary clinics and janitorial supply stores. There are many enzyme products available. Two that I particularly like that are available nationwide are Outright Pet Odor Eliminator® made by the Bramton Company and Nature's Miracle®.

I have had experience with both products and find that they both work well. I tend to favor Outright because I successfully used it in my former business and personally (thanks to Zack, my 17-pound bengal cat) for 15 years.

Do not be fooled into believing that you can spray on a deodorizer and the odor will magically disappear. It won't happen, and you will have wasted time and money on a product that doesn't work. Now let's get to the basics of pet odor removal.

First, Remove and Blot

You must remove any solid waste from the area and blot up any liquid residue using a heavy pad, paper towels or old, disposable rags. Lay this pad on the carpet and stand on it to absorb as much liquid as possible.

Step Two, Treat

Now you are ready to treat the accident with the enzyme product of your choice. Read the directions on the product carefully, following them exactly. Do not be afraid to really saturate the carpet. Generally, pet accidents soak through the carpet back and into the pad, so the enzyme treatment needs to soak in just as deeply. Water will not hurt your carpet; it is dipped in water numerous times during the dyeing process. Not putting the enzyme in deeply enough will not eliminate the odor. This is the most important step, so be sure to saturate the entire area, covering the circumference of the stain thoroughly, too. Remember, the urine goes into the carpet deeply and spreads

The Secret

Cover the treated area with a plastic garbage bag or a dry cleaner's bag. If there is any lettering on the bag do not let it touch the carpet or it will transfer to the carpet. Weight the plastic down with something heavy—the idea is to keep the enzyme from drying out until it can do its job, which is digesting the protein in the urine or feces. Leave the plastic in place at least 24 hours, preferably 48 hours—resist temptation, don't peek!

Step Three

Uncover the area and allow it to dry thoroughly. This may require as much as a week to 10 days, depending on how deeply you treated the spot. To speed drying, let a fan blow across the area.

Step Four

Once the area is completely dry (and only then), check for odor. If there is still odor, re-treat as directed above. If the odor is gone, clean the area with a good-quality carpet spotter that specializes in pet stains. I like Spot Shot Instant Carpet Stain Remover®. I have used it for years; and it works quickly and efficiently and won't leave residue in the carpet to encourage re-soiling.

If you have pets, keep some enzyme cleaner and carpet spotter on hand for pet accident emergencies.

Don't Panic If You Have No Enzyme or Carpet Spotter!

There is hope even if you don't have an enzyme product on hand. First, soak up as much liquid as possible from the carpet and remove any solids. If you have club soda on hand, pour that on and blot by standing on paper towels or rags (if you have no club soda, then use cold water). Do this repeatedly to remove as much urine as possible. Mix a mild solution of white vinegar and water (⅓ cup vinegar in a 1-quart bottle filled with cool water) in a spray bottle and spray onto pet stains to help remove the smell. Rinse with clear water and blot. Now go to the store at the earliest possible moment and buy the enzyme product and spotter and use as discussed previously.

Oops! The Carpet Changed Color

Urine spots may change the carpet color. The carpet may be lightened or bleached. Many times this is not obvious until the carpet is cleaned the first time after the accident. It is more common when the stain has not been treated in an appropriate manner. If this happens, try sponging the area with a mild ammonia solution. This will sometimes return the carpet to its original color or at least make it less noticeable.

Pet Accidents on Upholstered Furniture

When pets have accidents on upholstered furniture, you must first be sure that the fabric can be cleaned and treated with water. Check the platform of the sofa or chair under the cushion to determine the cleaning code. It should be listed on a tag. W indicates that the piece can be cleaned with water, so it can be treated as described on page 50. Clean the area using a good-quality upholstery spotting product. If the code is an S, this means solvent must be used in the cleaning process and this must be done by a professional. Do not apply an enzyme product or spotter. Call a professional. In this instance, the foam in the cushion may require replacing after cleaning.

If a pet urinates on a mattress, treat it as described on pages 70-72, but when done treating with the enzyme, cover the spot with plastic and stand the mattress on edge to expedite drying. If possible, leave the enzyme on for 12 hours.

Remove the plastic and sprinkle the area with borax. Let dry thoroughly and vacuum well. If necessary, follow by cleaning with a good-quality carpet spotter.

When the Cat Leaves You a Hairball or the Spaghetti Doesn't Agree with the Dog

If you have pets, you know what it's like when your cat or dog suffers a digestive upset. You hear the problem begin and run to move the dog or cat off the carpet (which seems to be their favorite place to leave "gifts"), but you're too late and faced with a mess to clean up.

First, resist the temptation to wipe up the mess. If there are solids that can be picked up with a paper towel, do so, but do not smear the accident into the carpet. Trying to wipe it up immediately will only make the mess worse. Instead, sprinkle a heavy coating of baking soda on the area and allow it to dry. The baking soda will absorb moisture and digestive acids. Once the area is dry, remove with paper towels or vacuum the area, removing all of the mess that will come up. Vacuum very thoroughly to remove the baking soda. Then and only then, you should grab the rag and the cleaner. Use your favorite carpet spotter, following the directions carefully. Remember to blot rather than rub.

If any discoloration remains after cleaning, try applying either undiluted lemon juice or hydrogen peroxide from the drugstore. Let it soak on the stain for 15 minutes and then blot. If the spot is still visible, apply again, watching carefully to be sure that there are no changes in carpet color. If you need a more aggressive treatment, mix lemon juice and cream of tartar into a thin paste. Apply to the spot, let dry and then vacuum up. When done with any of these procedures, rinse the carpet with cool water.

Removing Pet Hair from Fabric

Sometimes the vacuum cleaner isn't enough to remove pet hair from upholstered furniture. If this is true in your case, try one of the following methods:

• Dampen a sponge and wipe over the furniture, rinsing the sponge as necessary.

• Wipe down with your hands while wearing rubber gloves.

• Wrap tape around hands and wipe, changing as needed.

• Wipe with dampened body-washing puff.

• Wipe with a used dryer fabric softener sheet.

Keeping Cats from Digging in Your House Plants

To keep your cat from digging in indoor flower pots, place a cotton ball dipped in oil of cloves just below the soil line.

If your pet is eating your house plants, here's a great product to try. It's called Bitter Apple and is simply sprayed on the plant leaves. It won't hurt the plant or your pet. Its bitter taste will immediately stop the pet from chewing on the plants. Try your local pet store.

Keeping Fleas Out of Dog Houses

To deter fleas, sprinkle salt in the crevices of the dog house.

If Your Pet Meets the Wrong End of a Skunk ...

If your pet meets the wrong end of a skunk, apply Massengill™ douche, mixed as directed on the box. Do this outside and do not rinse. To help avoid eyes, apply a little petroleum jelly around the eye area.

14

Baby, Oh Baby and Kid's Corner

Kids are life's reward and add great joy to our lives. They also test all of our patience and cleaning skills. If you have children, large or small, or you have grandchildren, you need to memorize this chapter, or at least know where this book is at all times!

Baby Shoes

To make baby shoes easy to polish, rub them with the cut side of a raw potato or some rubbing alcohol prior to polishing. After polishing, spray with hair spray to keep the polish from rubbing off so easily. Put a little clear nail polish on the areas that are always scuffed and the shoes won't wear as much in those areas.

Bath Helpers

Put small slivers of mild soap into the open end of a small sock and tie shut, or make a small slit in a small size sponge and insert soap. These won't slip out of small hands (or yours when washing the baby).

For a great safe way to bathe a toddler, put a plastic laundry basket with mesh openings in the tub and put the child in it. It's a safe answer to bathing in the tub. But remember: Never leave a child alone in the bathtub.

Diaper Pins

If you are using cloth diapers, you know the misery of a dull diaper pin. To keep pins safely in one place where you can easily grab them and make them slide through fabric easily, store them stuck into a bar of soap.

Meal Mess Helper

To avoid those messy spills under baby's high chair, put a plastic tablecloth under it at mealtime. Cleanup will be a breeze and you can even put the tablecloth in the washing machine with an old towel, detergent and warm water. Hang to dry. This is a great tip when your toddler eats in Grandma's dining room!

Cleaning Stuffed Animals

Dust heavily with baking soda or cornstarch and work in well with your fingers. Roll the toys in towels or place in a plastic bag and leave overnight. The next day use a clean brush to brush the toys thoroughly after removing from the bag. Doing this outdoors saves cleanup.

Rattles and Teethers

A great place to wash these is in the dishwasher. Tie them in the top basket and wash with the dishes.

Formula Stains

On white clothes, apply undiluted lemon juice and lay the garment in the sun.

On colored clothes, make a paste of unseasoned meat tenderizer and cool water or an enzyme product from the laundry section at the grocery store. Apply and let sit for at least 30 minutes prior to laundering. Rubbing with a bar of wet Fels-Naptha Soap® will also help.

Cleaning Training Pants

To keep training pants white and odor-free, soak in a solution of 2 tablespoons of borax (available in the laundry section at the grocery store) and 1 gallon of hot water. Soak 1 hour prior to laundering.

To Remove Gum or Silly Putty™ from Hair

Rub cold cream or petroleum jelly into the gum. Use a dry Turkish towel-type rag to pull down on the hair strands and petroleum jelly. Work until all is out, then double shampoo. That old reliable peanut butter also works great. Massage the gum and peanut butter together between your fingers until the gum is loosened and can be removed. Freeze the area with ice cubes in a plastic bag and then pick out the gum.

Crayon on Walls

Spray with WD-40™ lubricant. Wipe off with a paper towel. Wash with hot water and liquid dishwashing detergent, working in a circular motion. Rinse well.

Crayon on Fabric

Place the stained surface down on a pad of paper towels and spray with WD-40™, let stand a few minutes, turn over and spray the other side.

Again, let sit a few minutes. Apply dishwashing detergent and work into the stained area, replacing the toweling as it absorbs the stain. Wash in the hottest water for the fabric you are working with, using your regular laundry detergent and all-fabric bleach.

Watercolor Paint on Fabric

Brush and rinse as much of the watercolor from the surface as possible. Apply a soft-scrubbing product with a damp sponge and rub in a circular motion, working toward the center of the spot. Rinse and dry. If any stain remains, apply nail polish remover to a cotton ball, blot the stain and rinse. Repeat as needed.

Watercolor Paint on Carpet

Apply rubbing alcohol with a sponge, blotting the stained area lightly. Turn the sponge as the stain is absorbed. Repeat until no more stain is being removed. Most of the remaining stain can be removed with a damp sponge and soft-scrubbing product. Rinse carpet well.

Marker Marks on Appliances, Wood or Hard Plastic

Wipe all stains with a damp sponge. If any stain remains, apply a soft-scrubbing product with a damp sponge, working in a circular motion, and rinse. If the stain remains, saturate a cotton ball with nail polish remover, blot the remaining stain and rinse well. This works on paneling, painted wood, tile and no-wax vinyl floors.

Marker on Carpet

Dampen a sponge with rubbing alcohol and use a blotting motion to absorb the marker, changing the sponge as needed. Apply a good carpet spotter, such as Spot Shot Carpet Stain Remover®, as directed on the can.

Marker on Clothing

Rinse the stain from the fabric with cold water until no more color is being removed. Place the fabric on paper towels and saturate with rubbing alcohol, using a cotton ball or small cloth to blot the stain. Replace the paper towels as often as needed to prevent re-staining the fabric. Treat the stain with a lather from a bar of Fels-Naptha Soap® and launder as usual.

Chalk on Hard Surfaces

For colored or white chalk on masonry, painted surfaces, vinyl flooring, tile, plastic and glass, brush and rinse as much of the chalk from the surface as possible. Remove the remaining stain with a damp sponge or cloth dipped in a soft-scrubbing product. Rinse surface well.

Chalk on Carpet

Vacuum the area well, using the attachment hose to concentrate the suction over the chalk. If stain remains, use a good carpet-spotting product.

Colored Chalk on Fabric

Place the stained area on a pad of paper towels and blot the spot with rubbing alcohol. Work in a lather of Fels-Naptha Soap® and launder as usual.

Glue on Carpet and Fabric

For water-based glue such as Elmer's™ School Glue, fold a paper towel to overlap the glue spot and saturate to almost dripping with warm water. Place this on the glue spot and leave on for about 45 minutes to an hour to allow the glue to soften. Rub the glue spot with a wet rag in a circular motion to remove all the glue you can. Repeat this procedure until glue is removed. Follow with a good carpet spotter.

Silly Putty™ Clay and Similar Products on Carpet and Fabric

Scrape off what you can with the dull edge of a knife. Spray with WD-40™ lubricant and let stand about 10-15 minutes. Scrape again. Respray as required, wiping up the stain with an old rag. Once you have removed the residue of the product, apply rubbing alcohol to the stain and blot, blot, blot. Reapply as necessary.

To remove from hard surfaces, spray with WD-40™ lubricant and wipe with a paper towel or old rag. Wipe any remaining stain with a cloth saturated with rubbing alcohol. Wash with a solution of dishwashing liquid and hot water, working in a circular motion. Rinse well.

Writing on Plastic Toys and Doll Faces

Ink and marker are very difficult to remove from plastic surfaces. Try applying a cotton ball saturated with rubbing alcohol. Let sit for 15 minutes and then rub. Sometimes using the pressure of a cotton swab dipped in alcohol helps. You can also try rubbing with a little cuticle remover on a soft cloth. Apply the cuticle remover, wait 10 minutes and then rub gently with the cloth.

15

The Nose Knows—
Odor Control

One thing I have found is that most people associate clean with what they smell. We want everything to smell clean. Here are some ideas that will perk your nose right up.

Product Corner

For those of you looking for a foolproof product you can purchase to use in eliminating all odors with success, I highly recommend the product ODORZOUT®.

This is a 100 percent natural product that stops many odors almost on contact—odors such as urine, mold, mildew, smoke, foot odor, skunk, paint and virtually every odor you can smell. It is made of blended natural zeolite minerals, contains no perfumes and is 100 percent safe for use around children or pets. You can even use it in the cat litterbox. In my testing, I have found no odor it didn't work on. Call 800-88STINK for more information or ordering, or visit the website: www.88stink.com.

Burned Food

Boil a few slices of lemon in a saucepan to clear the air of the smell of burned food.

Fried Food

This works on any fried food odor, but the next time you fry fish, be sure to try it. Place a small bowl of white vinegar next to the stove when you fry foods. The odor seems to disappear.

Refrigerators

To deodorize refrigerators, leave a bowl filled with clean clay cat litter or charcoal on the shelf to absorb odors. This is particularly helpful in refrigerators that are going to be shut off or moved. Make sure you leave the door partially open at all times to allow air circulation, and put some litter or charcoal in an old nylon stocking and tie the top shut. Lay this in the refrigerator and it will control odors. For strong odors, nothing works better than dry, fresh coffee grounds. Put them in a bowl and leave in the refrigerator until odor disappears. This can be used in conjunction with the cat litter or charcoal very effectively.

Cars

If you smoke in the car, put a layer of baking soda in the bottom of the ashtray to absorb smoke odor. Empty it frequently. Dryer fabric softener sheets placed under the seats also help to keep the smoke smell under control. For musty smells, put cat litter in a nylon stocking, tie the top shut and place several under the seats or in the trunk.

Wood Trunks, Dressers and Chests

Many times old wood trunks and dressers will have a musty mildew or old odor. To eliminate this take a slice of white bread (yes, it has to be white), put it in a bowl and cover with white vinegar. Leave enclosed in the trunk or drawers for 24 hours. If odor remains, repeat the process. If mildew odor persists in dresser drawers, shellac or varnish the inside of them and odor will be sealed in and eliminated.

Home Odors

Wintergreen oil is a wonderful deodorant. Purchase some at a health food store and put a few drops on cotton balls and stash in plants, decorative pieces, etc., around the house.

Make Your Own Air Freshener

In a gallon jug combine 1 cup baking soda, ¼ cup clear ammonia and 1 tablespoon scent (use your imagination—any scented oils or extracts work). Slowly add 16 cups of warm water, label and store. To use, pour well-shaken solution into a spray container and mist air as needed.

16

Hot Tips for Irons and Ironing Boards

Cleaning an Iron That Does Not Have a Nonstick Surface

Heat the iron to the hot, nonsteam setting. Run it over table salt sprinkled on a brown paper grocery bag.

You can also use non-gel toothpaste. Apply it to a damp cloth and rub over the soleplate on a cool iron until starch buildup and ironing residue are removed. Rinse well.

For terrible buildup, burned-on fabric or starch, take the iron outside and cover all parts of the iron except soleplate with paper. Spray oven cleaner directly onto the soleplate of a cool iron. Wait several minutes and then rinse off well with cool water and an old rag or sponge.

With a Nonstick Surface

Use laundry pre-spotter. Rub on and rinse off well.

After Cleaning

After cleaning your iron with any of these methods, remember to rinse it well and then fill with water, heat on the heavy steam setting and iron over old fabric prior to using on clothes. This will remove any residue remaining in the vent holes.

Cleaning the Vent Holes

Many times the vent holes in the bottom of the iron will become clogged. Take a pipe cleaner and clean out each hole individually.

Always empty steam irons after each use to prevent clogging.

Cleaning the Internal Parts

Fill the steam iron with equal portions of water and white vinegar. Let it steam for several minutes. Disconnect the iron and let it sit for one hour. Empty and rinse with clear water using the same process. Be sure to iron over old fabric prior to ironing clothes.

Keeping Ironing Board Covers Clean

To make covers last longer and stay clean longer, spray them with spray starch once the cover is on the board and iron the starch in well.

Energy-Efficient Ironing

Put aluminum foil under the ironing board cover when you put it on the board. It will reflect heat onto the garments as you iron and cut ironing time.

⓲
Taking Charge of Electronic Equipment

Telephones

To clean and disinfect telephone receivers, apply Listerine™ mouthwash with a soft cotton pad or rag. Do not rinse off. This is great advice for offices during cold and flu season.

Television Screens

Denatured alcohol (available at hardware stores) makes a great cleaner for many pieces of electronic equipment. To clean the TV screen, turn off the power to the TV. Apply alcohol to a rag or paper towel and wipe the screen thoroughly, then buff.

Stop Dust from Settling

Apply antistatic product to a rag and wipe the screen and cabinet, or mix 1 part liquid fabric softener to 4 parts water and apply with a soft cloth and buff.

Radios

These need to be dusted often. Clean them occasionally with denatured alcohol applied with a cotton ball. Do not use alcohol on wood.

Cameras

Cameras should always be stored in their cases when not in use. This prevents them from becoming dusty. Except for wiping off the outside of the lens with a cotton ball and a little alcohol, leave cleaning to the professionals.

Videocassette Recorders

These need to be kept free of dust to stay in good working order. It is best to cover them with a plastic cover when not in use. If the room is damp, keep silica packets (available from florists or many times found in new leather shoes or purses) on top of the VCR (keep these packets away from children). Clean the VCR occasionally using a cleaning tape to ensure good-quality pictures on playback. Store videotapes in cardboard or plastic cases to keep them clean and in good condition for playback or recording.

Answering Machines

These need to be dusted with a lambswool duster, particularly inside the machine. You can use an aerosol cleaner, but make sure that the machine is dry before you replace the cassette.

Fax Machines

These also need to be kept dusted and occasionally wiped with denatured alcohol.

Compact Discs

To keep your compact discs clean, mix 2 tablespoons of baking soda and 1 pint of water in a spray bottle. Shake well to mix and spray on the disc, wiping with a soft cloth. Do not wipe in a circular motion; wipe from the center hole in the disc out to the outside edge.

Computers

To avoid costly problems with computers, it is important that they be kept dust-free. Dust between the keys of your keyboard with a cotton swab, or vacuum with the duster-brush on your vacuum or with a special computer vacuum that helps you get between the keys.

Mix 1 part water and 1 part alcohol and apply to the keys

with a cotton swab. Don't overwet. Undiluted denatured alcohol may also be used in the same manner.

Dust the screen and spray with an antistatic product.

Make sure that computers are situated out of direct sunlight, which can cause overheating. Sunlight also makes it difficult for the user to see the computer screen clearly.

A Special Reminder

Never clean any electronic equipment without unplugging it first!

18

The Care and Hanging of Pictures and Paintings

Pictures and paintings are part of the personal touches that make a house a home. Here are some ideas for hanging and cleaning pictures and oil and acrylic paintings.

Finding the Stud the Easy Way

When you are ready to hang a picture, especially a heavy one, it is a good idea to find a stud to hang it from. Take an electric razor and run it across the wall. You will notice a distinct difference in the sound of the razor going over a hollow wall and the sound when it hits a stud. Use this whenever you need to find the stud to hang anything around the house.

Keeping Cockeyed Pictures Straight

Wind some adhesive tape around the center of the picture wire. The wire will be less likely to slip on the hanger.

Place masking tape on the back four corners of your picture and press against the wall. Wrap masking tape, sticky side out, around the middle of a round toothpick and place a few near the bottom, backside of the frame.

Preventing Experimental Holes

Cut a paper pattern of each picture or mirror that you plan to hang and pin to the wall. After you've found the correct positions for the hangers, perforate the paper with a sharp pencil to mark the wall.

When you want to avoid nail holes in the walls, hang pictures with a sewing machine needle. They hold up to 30 pounds and leave almost no marks on the wall.

Staining Unfinished Picture Frames

Stain them beautifully with ordinary liquid shoe polish. Apply one coat and let dry. Follow with another coat, then wax with a good paste wax. Brown shoe polish gives the wood a walnut glow and oxblood emulates a mahogany or cherry color. Tan polish will look like a light maple. This hides scratches, too.

Cleaning Glass-Covered Pictures

Never spray any cleaner directly on the glass; it may seep under and onto the picture. Spray a paper towel with window cleaner, wipe and polish with a dry towel.

Polish glass with a used fabric softener sheet to shine and deter dust.

Cleaning Oil and Acrylic Paintings

Give them an occasional dusting with a clean, lint-free cloth or a soft brush. Spot-clean if necessary with a barely damp rag or piece of white bread. If the painting is worth a lot of money or has sentimental value, take it to a professional. Even a soft dust cloth can snag and cause a chip.

Gilt Picture Frames

Remove stains from gilt picture frames by rubbing gently with a cloth moistened in milk.

Photo Emergency

If you have a picture that is stuck to the glass, immerse the glass and the photo in a pan of room-temperature water and keep testing until the photo pulls free. Don't try to rush it! Let the photo air-dry. Since most photo prints get a water bath during processing, there shouldn't be any damage, though this is not a 100 percent guarantee.

19
Paint by Numbers

One of the questions men ask me most frequently is how to get through the job of painting quickly and make it easier. Actually, there are things you can do to make the job go much more smoothly.

Short-term Storage

If you need to store a paintbrush or roller in the middle of a project or between coats of paint, place it in a tightly sealed plastic bag and place in the freezer. The brush or roller will not dry out for a day or two and no cleanup is needed until you have completed the project.

Protect Hardware

When painting woodwork, cover door knobs, locks and other hardware with a generous coat of petroleum jelly. If the paint splashes where it shouldn't, it can easily be wiped up.

Splatter Removal

For easy removal of paint splatters on window panes, use a round typewriter eraser with a brush on the end—it's safer than a razor and easy, too!

Painting Screws

To make painting screws from hardware easier, stick them in a piece of foam packing material. The screw heads will all be facing up, ready to be sprayed or painted in one coat.

Cleaning Hands

Use vegetable oil to clean oil-based paints off hands. The oil is safer than paint thinner, has no fumes and is mild to the skin. After using the oil, wash well with soap.

Preventing White Paint from Yellowing

To stop white paint from yellowing with age, put several drops of black paint in for every quart of white paint. Mix very well.

Keep Cans Clean

Cover the rim of the paint can with masking tape if you are going to pour paint from the can. When you are done, remove the tape to clean the top.

Drip Realignment

If you are painting from the can, punch two or three nail holes in the small groove in the top rim of your paint can. As you wipe the paint from your brush on the rim, the paint will drip back into the can instead of collecting in the groove and spilling over and down the sides of the can.

Clean Brushes in a Second

To make a paintbrush easier to clean, wrap masking tape around the metal ferrule and about ½ inch over the bristles. Rather than drying on the bristles, paint will collect on the masking tape. To clean, remove the tape and clean the paint that remains on the brush.

Garbage Garment

Wear a garbage bag as a cover-all when painting overhead. Cut a hole for head and arms. You can cover your head with an old shower cap. No more paint splatters on clothes and hair!

Easier-Opening Cans

When sealing the lid on a paint can, wipe a thin layer of petroleum jelly around the rim. This will allow the can to open easily the next time.

Record-Keeping

Before you store leftover paint, list the rooms you have painted with it on the can. Touch-ups are easier if you don't have to try to figure out which can of paint you used for what.

Paint-Catching Wristband

If you paint like I do and have runs of paint going down your arms every time you paint over your head, wrap an old washcloth around your wrist, secure with a rubber band and remove and throw away when you are done painting.

Dry Brushes Completely

If you soak your brush between painting sessions, be sure to drain out all of the liquid or you will have a dripping mess when you start painting again. One good way to do this is to stand the brush straight up in an empty can for a few min-

utes to let the fluid drip out or suspend it from a stick laid across the top of an empty can that is taller than the brush. To be absolutely sure that the brush is dry, take an old rag, wrap it around the brush and squeeze the bristles from the top downward over the can.

Where to Start

Start painting at the top of the wall and work your way down. That way, if paint drips down it can be smoothed out as you go.

When to Start

No need to get up early to paint outside. You don't want to start painting until after the morning dew has evaporated. But, remember, never paint in the direct sunlight.

⓴
The Grill Drill

L et's talk about ways to make cooking on the grill easier
and more fun.

Prevent Sticking

Before you light the barbecue, spray the grill rack with nonstick cooking spray. This works great on gas or charcoal

grills. Apply a liberal coat and food won't stick, making cooking and cleanup a lot easier.

Cleaning the Grill

To clean the grill surface when it is heavily caked with baked-on food, follow this procedure. Simply wrap the rack in a piece of heavy-duty aluminum foil, dull side facing out. Heat the barbecue to high heat and place the rack over the coals or flame for approximately 10 to 12 minutes. When you remove the foil after it has cooled, all the burned-on grease and food drippings will fall off and your rack will be spotless and ready to grill again.

Immediately After Cooking

Make a ball of aluminum foil and "scrub" the warm grill rack surface with it, taking care not to burn your fingers.

The Bathtub Method and a Less-Messy Version

Many people recommend putting the grill rack in the bathtub filled with hot water, detergent and ammonia. I find this a particularly messy way to do it because you have to clean the tub when you're done. If you do use this method, be sure to lay old rags or a garbage bag in the tub to prevent scratching the tub surface with the grill rack.

I suggest you try this method instead. Lay some paper towels moistened with undiluted ammonia on both sides of the rack. Put it in an appropriate-size plastic bag and seal.

Leave it overnight and the next day open the bag, away from your face—it stinks. Wipe down with the paper towels in the bag, wash with soapy water and rinse.

Keeping Pan Bottoms Clean

Before setting a pan on the grill rack to warm barbecue sauce or cook additional foods, rub the pan bottom with bar soap and it will be easier to clean the soot off when you are done.

Cleaning Permanent Briquettes

Flip the briquettes occasionally and ignite the grill with the cover closed. Allow it to burn at a high setting for about 15 minutes.

Grease Splatters

For cement or wood patios, keep a container of salt nearby when barbecuing. Should grease spatter or drip, immediately cover with salt. Sweep up and reapply until grease is absorbed. Scrub with dishwashing liquid and rinse.

Keeping the Outside of the Grill Clean

This is such a fast, easy way to clean the outside of the grill. It works well on charcoal and gas grills and will make them look almost like new. Take some Go-Jo Waterless Hand Cleaner® (available at grocery stores, hardware stores and home centers) and rub it on the outside of a cool grill with an old rag or paper towel. Work it into the metal well, paying special attention to any grease or barbecue sauce spots. Do not rinse; instead, take paper towels and buff the grill surface and watch as the dirt is replaced by a great shine.

Keeping the Glass Grill Window Clean

Many gas grills have glass windows in them. Of course, once you use the grill a few times you can no longer see through the window! To clean this, spray the inside of the glass with oven cleaner. Wait a few minutes and then scrub and rinse well. On the outside of the glass use Go-Jo Waterless Hand Cleaner® and buff well.

21

Everything Under the Sun for Patio Furniture

No matter what part of the country you live in, at some time you have to clean the outdoor furniture. Follow this advice to make the job go faster.

Furniture Cushions

There are several ways to clean outdoor furniture cushions. You can use Spot Shot Upholstery Stain Remover® or Spot Shot Instant Carpet Stain Remover®. Follow the directions on the can. Or, mix your own solution. In a spray bottle combine 1 teaspoon of dishwashing liquid and 1 teaspoon of borax per quart of warm water. Spray this on the cushion on both sides and let it sit for about 15 minutes. Then take out the hose and, using a strong spray, rinse the solution and the dirt off the cushions. Put them back on the chairs and set them out of the direct sun to dry. Once they have dried to just damp, apply a good coating of Scotchgard™ Fabric Protector® (available at grocery stores and home centers) to protect the cushions and make cleaning easier the next time. Vacuum the cushions as needed to remove dust between cleanings.

Aluminum

Although it doesn't rust, aluminum can become dull and pitted when left outdoors. To clean and restore the shine, scrub the frames with a plastic scrubber soaked in detergent or a soap-filled steel wool pad, then rinse and dry.

Aluminum with Baked-Enamel Finish

Use a sponge soaked in detergent and wash well, rinse and dry. To protect, apply a coat of good-quality car wax. This will make cleaning easier and maintain the shine. It can be used on tables with a baked-enamel finish, too.

Canvas

Soiled canvas seats and chair backs are usually machine washable, but be sure to put them back on the furniture when they are still damp to maintain their shape. To clean canvas that you cannot put in the washing machine, such as large seats, backs or awnings, run a scrub brush back and forth across a bar of Fels-Naptha Soap®. Rub this back and forth across the canvas and then rinse well. This will even remove bird droppings and, many times, the staining, too.

Plastic

Wash with good all-purpose cleaner and water, then rinse with water and dry. An alternative for white furniture is automatic dishwasher detergent and warm water (1 gallon warm water to 3 tablespoons automatic dishwasher detergent). Wash and let solution sit on the furniture for 15 minutes or so and then rinse and dry.

Maintaining Shine

To maintain the shine on plastic, resin and metal furniture, apply a good-quality paste car wax just as you would when waxing a car.

22

All Hands on Decks

A certain amount of routine maintenance is required to keep your backyard deck structurally sound, safe and looking its best.

Though other types of lumber may have been used, chances are that your deck is built of cedar, redwood or pressure-treated yellow pine. These are the most commonly used materials for decks because they are resistant to rot and insect damage. When exposed to the elements for extended periods of time, any wood will show signs of weathering. Even if the deck was originally treated with stain or a preservative, this treatment eventually needs to be renewed.

Inspect and Protect

The first thing you need to do once the weather turns nice is inspect the deck surfaces for any splintering, which you will need to sand. Pay special attention to the railing.

You'll find many stains and sealers designed for decks. Several manufacturers now offer products called deck brighteners, which actually bleach the surface to remove stains and weathering on wood surfaces. Apply these products carefully, following the instructions. Usually you will brush the product on with a stiff bristle brush, and rinse off thoroughly prior to applying any finish coating.

Sealers protect the deck from moisture and are available in clear or tinted varieties to act as a stain. Sealers require periodic renewal to maintain protection.

Now go over the actual decking to be sure it is tight and in place, fixing whatever is required. Finally, if no repair or staining is needed, follow some of these suggestions to give the deck a good cleaning.

If there are leaves and other debris on the deck, either sweep or use a blower to remove it.

Hose Off the Deck

With a garden hose and a strong—and preferably long-handled—brush, use the strongest spray setting on the nozzle to break up dirt on the surface. Follow this with the brush to loosen any stubborn soil. This works especially well with two people, who can take turns hosing and scrubbing.

Kill Mildew

Check the condition of the wood. Green or black areas indicate mold and mildew. To remove mold and mildew from the wood you will need either a commercial deck-cleaning product (which may be purchased at your local home center) or you can prepare your own using a mixture of 1 cup trisodium phosphate (available at janitorial supply stores and home centers), 1 gallon of oxygen-type bleach (safer to use than chlorine bleach) and 1 gallon of hot water. The bleach will kill the mildew and the TSP will thoroughly clean the wood surface. You can apply this with a garden sprayer or mop it on.

First wet down the deck with the hose and then apply the cleaning solution. Spread the solution evenly and scrub with the brush you used earlier. Let the solution sit for about 15 minutes and then hose off. Repeat the wetting, bleaching and rinsing process as necessary until the entire deck is clean. Make sure you do stairs, handrails and any other deck parts.

After you have done the entire deck, I recommend that you hose down the grass and any plants surrounding it to remove any solution that has dripped on them. No damage should be done to plants, but rinsing is a good precaution. If you have used a garden sprayer, be sure to wash it out well and rinse the brush before storing.

Quick Cleaning

To give the deck a quick cleaning during the use season, mix up a gallon of hot water and ¼ cup of any good-quality household cleaner, or 1 gallon of hot water, 1 tablespoon of dishwashing liquid and ¼ cup of borax. Mop the deck down with one of these solutions and rinse well. Again, be sure to rinse plants and grass down.

Removing Sap from an Unfinished Wood Deck

Tree sap can be a problem on wood decks. To remove it, apply mineral spirits with an old rag, rub and wash off with dishwashing liquid and water (1 teaspoon of dishwashing liquid to 1 quart of hot water). Rinse well.

Concrete Solutions for Cleaning Cement Driveways and Patios

One question everyone asks is how to clean cement driveways, garage floors and patios. The best time to clean cement is when the temperature is between 50 and 75 degrees and the direct sun is not shining on it. Take this into consideration when using the cleaning methods in this chapter.

Grab the Dust on Cement

To make quick work of sweeping a cement garage floor or patio, pick up some sweeping compound at either a janitorial supply store, hardware store or home center. The sweeping compound will "grab" the dust instead of spreading it in the air as you sweep. When you're done, just sweep it into a dust pan and throw out.

Kitty Litter™— a Garage Floor's Best Friend

Cat box litter, either regular clay or clumping, is wonderful for absorbing liquid spills, especially oil of any kind. Simply pour it on the spot and then—the secret to success—grind it into the spot with your foot. Leave it and allow it to absorb all of the oil that it can. Then sweep up. Repeat the process if necessary.

Old Stains on Cement

Apply a spray-and-wash product and leave it on for 5-10 minutes. Sprinkle with laundry detergent, scrub with a stiff brush or broom and then rinse.

Another good method is to make a paste of hot water and automatic dishwasher detergent. Scrub it into the spot and let it soak for at least one hour or overnight. Add additional water and scrub, then rinse well.

Removing the Toughest Stains

Use oven cleaner to remove the toughest spots. Spray it on, keeping your face well back. Let it stand for 15 minutes and then scrub with a stiff brush or broom and hose off. Repeat if necessary. Do not allow children or pets in the area when using this method. Rinse cement and brush with plenty of water. Do not combine other cleaning products with the oven cleaner until it is rinsed well with water.

Removing Rust from Concrete

Wet the concrete and sprinkle with lemon Kool-Aid™. Cover with plastic and soak for 15 minutes. Remove plastic, scrub with a brush and rinse well.

Another method that may work for you is applying ZUD Heavy Duty Cleanser®. This can be purchased at the store in the cleanser section. Make a paste with warm water and work in well with a brush. Let soak for 30 minutes and then scrub with additional hot water and rinse well.

If the rust stain is really bad, you will have to use a solution of 10 parts water to 1 part muriatic acid. Let this sit 2-3 hours and then scrub with a stiff (nonmetallic) brush. Use extreme caution if you use this method. Wear goggles, gloves and old clothes, and rinse, rinse, rinse! Keep children and pets away from the area while using the acid.

At the Carwash

Auto Quick Tips

Stain guard

Before long trips, spray the front of your car, where the bugs collect, with nonstick cooking spray. This will stop bugs from sticking, and bugs and dirt can be easily washed off.

Cleaning the windshield

Clean your windshield with baking soda and water prior to washing the car. White vinegar added to a wet, lint-free rag will remove grease film and give you a streak-free shine.

Bug scraper

Save the plastic net bags from produce such as onions to scrub the window when it is spattered with bugs. Keep a couple in the car to use at the gas station when washing your windows and then throw them away. Great to have on hand when you're traveling.

Removing tar

Saturate tar spots with linseed oil. Let soak and then rub with an old rag or paper towel moistened with the oil.

Removing bumper stickers

Use a blow-dryer to heat the sticker, then use a flat edge, such as an old credit card, and start peeling. Continue to heat and peel. Remove residue with nail polish remover.

Chrome

If you have dirty chrome on your car, simply dampen a piece of aluminum foil and rub. This is a great way to remove rust, too.

Battery corrosion stopper

Scrub the battery terminals and the holder with ½ cup of baking soda combined with 2 cups warm water. When dry, apply petroleum jelly to the area.

Preventing doors from freezing

Spray the rubber gaskets around the door and trunk with nonstick cooking spray. This will keep water out and also keep the gaskets supple. Remember this trick if you plan on having the car washed in cold weather.

Making windshield washer solvent

This can be used in the windshield washer container in your car—winter or summer. It will not freeze and is a great cleaner. Combine 1 quart rubbing alcohol, 1 cup water and 2 tablespoons of liquid dishwashing detergent or laundry detergent. This should not freeze even at 30 degrees below zero.

Removing salt residue from carpet

Combine a 50-50 solution of white vinegar and water. Apply to carpet and blot. Reapply as necessary.

General interior cleaning

For spots on carpet and upholstery, count on a good carpet spotter such as Spot Shot Instant Carpet Stain Remover®. Use as directed on the can.

For leather upholstery

Wet a soft cloth with warm water and rub it across a wet bar of Dove Moisturizing Soap® several times. Wash the seats thoroughly, rinsing out the cloth and reapplying the soap as it becomes soiled. Do not rinse; instead, dry with a soft cloth.

Professional Interior Cleaning

To really give your car a complete cleaning, rent an extraction machine at the hardware store or home center and clean upholstered seats and carpet thoroughly. Be sure to leave the windows down to allow the interior to dry completely.

25

Do Away with Window Pains

To achieve professional results you need to use the same tools the professionals use. You can find all of these things at either a janitorial supply store (look in the yellow pages) or a hardware store.

Use the Right Tools

Squeegee

A good squeegee is an absolute must. Don't be fooled into thinking that a cheap plastic squeegee or a car windshield squeegee will do the job—they won't! The best size to start with is a 12- or 14-inch squeegee. This will work well on most windows, and once you have mastered this size you can move up to an 18-inch for large-paned windows and down to a 6-inch for small French panes.

Scrubber

A good scrubber is a plus. This tool looks like a squeegee wearing a fluffy coat. It is used to wet and clean the window prior to using the squeegee. If you do not want to invest in this, be sure you buy a good natural sponge.

Rag or Chamois

Use a dry rag or chamois for drying the squeegee rubber (blade) and the edges of the glass.

Scraper

Use a window scraper for removing paint, concrete and other stubborn debris. If you don't purchase this you can use a good medium- to fine-grade steel wool pad. If you use this be sure the pad and the window are soapy wet. Never use one of those scrub pads that you use on dishes; this will scratch the glass. Never use steel wool on tinted glass.

Extension Pole

If you have difficult, high, hard to reach windows, you might consider an extension pole made for a squeegee. This will enable you to stand on the ground and reach the high windows without a ladder.

Bucket and TSP

A bucket of water and TSP, trisodium phosphate, or dishwashing detergent (2 or 3 squirts to a bucket) added after you have filled the bucket with water.

Let's Get Started

Fill your bucket with warm water and add the TSP or dishwashing liquid.

Be sure you have all the necessary equipment laid out and ready for use.

Follow the steps listed below, in order. You'll be cleaning like a pro in no time!

Dip your scrubber or sponge into the cleaning solution and wash the window thoroughly, using a very wet steel wool pad to remove any stubborn spots, such as bug stains. You do not have to press too hard on the steel wool pad. Rewet the window so you will have time to squeegee the window before it dries. Try not to clean in the direct sunlight, as it will cause streaking and spotting.

Tilt the squeegee at an angle so that 2 inches of rubber blade touches the glass. Start at the top corner and draw the squeegee along the top edge of the window.

Wipe the squeegee blade on a sponge, start on the dry surface close to the frame and draw the squeegee down to within about 3 inches of the bottom of the glass.

Repeat this stroke until you have squeegeed all of the glass. Be sure you overlap each stroke and wipe the squeegee blade after each stroke.

Soak up excess water with a well-rinsed sponge.

Do the same thing you did in step two at the top of the glass, this time working at the bottom of the glass.

Have your rag or chamois handy to wipe the window edges if needed. If you see a streak on the window, let it dry, then use poly/cotton rag, such as an old T-shirt, to polish it out.

Spray-and-Wipe Cleaning Solutions

If you prefer to wash your windows the spray-and-wipe way, here are a couple of good cleaning solutions.

Polishing Glass or Removing Screen and Bug Stains

Make a thin paste of baking soda and water, rub onto glass, rinse well and dry with a soft cloth.

Easy Window Cleaner

Combine:

> 2 quarts warm water
> ½ cup cornstarch

Apply to window with a sponge and buff dry with paper towels or soft, lint-free rags.

Tough-Job Window Cleaner

Combine:

> 1 pint rubbing alcohol
> 2 tablespoons clear ammonia
> 2 tablespoons dishwashing liquid

Apply to the window using a nylon covered sponge, rinse and buff dry. Great for hard-water spots.

Screen Savers

Most people just hose screens down to clean them. This just moves the dirt from one part of the screen to the other. Here's a better way. Just soap the screen with a sponge dipped in a pail of warm water containing 2 tablespoons of dishwashing liquid, ¼ cup of ammonia and 2 tablespoons of borax. Really suds up the screen. Now lay a rag on the ground and gently tap the screen on it. Most of the soapy water containing the dirt will come off this way. To finish, rinse the screen with the hose and stand to dry, or rag dry.

Bad News

Remember, no matter what you have heard about cleaning windows with newspaper, don't do it. It is a dirty, messy way and leaves newsprint all over white window trim and paint.

QUICK TIP ....
Use a dry blackboard eraser on a dry window or mirror after cleaning to banish any streaks you've left behind!

㉖
Flower Power

Making Fresh Flowers Last Longer

To make fresh flowers from your garden or floral arrangements from the florist last longer, use the following recipe. Remove any foliage below the waterline, trim the stem ends periodically and keep the solution fresh and your flowers will live longer.

Combine:

1 quart of water

2 tablespoons of lemon juice

1 tablespoon sugar

½ teaspoon liquid bleach

Add the solution to the flower container and enjoy. If you have an arrangement from the florist, add this solution each time you add water.

If you don't have the above ingredients on hand, add 2 ounces of Listerine™ mouthwash per gallon of water.

To make cut flowers last longer without shedding, spray with hair spray. Hold the spray can about a foot away from the flowers and spray in an upward direction to prevent the flowers from drooping.

Cleaning Vases

To easily clean a flower vase, fill with warm water and add one or two denture-cleaning tablets, depending on the size of the vase. Let it soak at least an hour or overnight. Wash, rinse and dry well. If you don't have any denture-cleaning tablets, throw in a handful of dry rice and some white vinegar and shake, shake, shake. Let soak with vinegar and warm water if necessary. Wash and rinse the vase well.

Transporting Fresh Flowers

If you are taking fresh flowers from your garden as a gift, or to the office, fill a balloon with water, put the stems in and secure the neck of the balloon to the stems with a rubber band, twist tie or ribbon. Poking the stems through a paper doily will also hold the stems in place and make an attractive presentation. Your flowers will arrive fresh-looking at their destination with no spilled water to worry about!

The Dirt on Flower Pots

When planting flowers in a pot with a drainage hole in the bottom, line the bottom of the pot with enough coffee filters to cover it. Add a few pebbles and then add the soil. When you water the plant the dirt won't run out the bottom.

Flower Filler

When planting shallow-rooted flowers in a large pot, line the bottom with coffee filters and pebbles, fill the pot ⅓ full of packing peanuts and then fill with soil. The pot will be much lighter to move and you won't require as much soil to fill the pot.

Healthful Water

When you boil eggs, save the water to water your plants. It is full of minerals.

Cold coffee or tea combined with water provides an acidic drink for your plants. (Be sure it doesn't run out on the carpet.)

Water from an aquarium provides excellent fertilizer for plants.

Club soda that has lost its fizz is good for plants.

Going on vacation? Stand plants in the sink or bathtub, depending on the number you have. Be sure they are in pots with a hole in the bottom. Add a few inches of water to the tub and plants will be automatically watered while you are gone. To preserve the tub finish, lay an old towel in the bottom to set plants on.

Unbugged

If bugs are a problem on indoor plants, spray the soil with insect spray and immediately cover the plant with a plastic bag. Leave in place for a couple of days and then uncover.

Let Them Shine

To shine indoor plant leaves, wipe gently with glycerin. Another great way to add shine is by wiping leaves with a mixture of half milk and half water. Do not use oil on plant leaves, as it attracts dust and dirt.

Window Boxes and Patio Flower Pots

These are easy to keep clean. After you plant the flowers in the pots, put a layer of gravel or marbles on top. When you water or it rains, the dirt won't splash all over the plants, pots, patio or porch.

Hanging Plants

To water hanging plants with ease and without the mess of water running all over, use ice cubes. The cubes melt slowly and won't allow water to run out onto the floor or patio.

Weed Prevention

To kill weeds growing in sidewalk cracks, pour boiling salt water on them. Use a mixture of ¼ cup salt to 2 quarts water. To prevent the weeds from growing in the cracks, sprinkle salt into the cracks.

Cleaning Artificial Flowers

To really clean and remove soil from artificial flowers, dried silk or polyester, place them in a bag with table salt. Add salt in proportion to the size of the flowers. Close the bag and shake the flowers in the salt for several minutes, or longer if the flowers are heavily soiled. Shake gently to remove the salt. The salt won't look dirty when you are done, but if you run water into it, you will be surprised how much dirt is removed from the flowers.

You can also place silk flowers in a pillowcase, tie a knot in it and put it in the clothes dryer on "air fluff" or "air only" for about 15 to 20 minutes.

Spray polyester flowers with acrylic spray from the craft store and they will resist soiling. If they get very dusty, wash under a mild stream of running water, shake and stand up to dry.

27

Bug Out— User-Friendly Pest Control

A re the bugs bugging you? Are the pests pestering you? You can control bugs without chemicals, the safe, environmentally friendly way. When planting flowers or controlling insects inside the house, keep this guide handy.

Insect Repellent

When using insect sprays, especially those containing DEET, try spraying clothes instead of skin—it's much safer, especially for children.

Or Try Vinegar

A wonderful substitute for insect repellent is white vinegar. Apply it to the skin with a cotton ball, applying liberally. Bugs hate the way you taste and the smell of the vinegar disappears once it dries. Great for kids!

Aphids

Mix nonfat dry milk with water according to the directions on the box, then put in a spray bottle and apply it to the leaves of your plants. As the milk dries, the aphids get stuck in the milky residue and die. You can rinse the plants from time to time with the hose. This will not harm your plants and offers an inexpensive solution to a big problem.

Aphids and Spiders

Wash off the plant with a mild solution of dishwashing liquid and water. Try a ratio of ½ teaspoon dishwashing liquid to 1 quart water. Flush leaves, including undersides, with the solution. Do not rinse off.

Aphids and Whiteflies

These bugs are attracted to bright yellow and can be trapped by placing a yellow board or other yellow objects such as yellow poster board, oleo lids, or sticks painted yellow, coated with heavy motor oil, petroleum jelly or Tack Trap® near susceptible plants. Recoat when the traps dry out.

Aphids on Roses

Use 1½ teaspoons of baking soda per pint of water and apply every seven days. This method is user-, earth- and child-friendly.

Grasshoppers

To deter grasshoppers, plant basil around the flower bed borders. Grasshoppers will eat the basil and leave the plants alone.

Ants

For ants on the counter, wipe the counter down with undiluted white vinegar.

To prevent ants from coming in the house, or getting into cupboards, sprinkle dried mint or red pepper where they are entering the house and in the cupboards.

To get rid of anthills, pour 3 gallons of boiling water down them. This is best done when the ants are active and near the surface. Do not do this close to flowers or they will die, too.

Another way to kill ants is to mix a combination of 50 percent borax and 50 percent confectioner's sugar. Place this on cardboard or a piece of board near the ant hill. The ants are attracted by the sugar and carry the fatal borax/sugar combination back to the nest to feed the queen and other ants. Soon all are dead. A note of caution: Do not place this where children or pets may ingest this mixture. Borax is sold in the laundry aisle at the grocery store as a laundry additive, not as a pesticide.

Cockroaches

To keep cockroaches out of the cupboards, place some bay leaves on the shelves.

Kill cockroaches with a mixture of ⅓ borax, ⅓ cornmeal, ⅓ flour and a dash of powdered sugar. Sprinkle this in crevices under sinks and vanities where cockroaches love to hide. Remember, keep this away from children and animals.

You can also try this formula for cockroaches: Mix powdered boric acid with sugar and powdered nondairy creamer. I use a mixture of 50 percent boric acid to 25 percent each sugar and creamer. This is inexpensive and relatively safe, but it should be kept away from children and pets. Sprinkle the mixture in all the dark, warm places that cockroaches love—under sinks and stoves, behind refrigerators, in cabinets and closets, and so on. The roaches will walk through the powder and then clean themselves, much the way a cat preens. Once they ingest the powder they die.

㉘
Putting Your
Best Foot Forward

What article of clothing gets more wear and tear than our shoes? Many of us have a favorite pair of tennis shoes that we live in. When we come home we take them off after a hot day at work, and our family leaves the room making comments about a skunk smelling better. Now, there is a quick, easy answer to shoe odor. Taking good care of shoes will make them look better, of course, but it will also extend the life of the shoes, too.

Cleaning and Deodorizing Shoes

This method will work with any shoe. First, sprinkle some baking soda in the shoe, then place it in a plastic bag and freeze it for a night or two. Allow the shoe to come to room temperature (unless you want to cool your feet) and then shake out the baking soda and wear. It is a good idea to leave the baking soda in the shoe until the next wearing.

Stretching Shoes

Here's another freezer tip for the pair of shoes that pinches your toes. For each shoe use a heavy-duty zip closure bag, or double up two of them and put them in each shoe. Carefully pour water into the bags, until the toe area is full. Close the bags securely so the water doesn't seep out and wet the shoes. To help prevent the outside of the shoes from getting wet, put each shoe in a plastic bag. Place the shoes in the freezer for at least 24 hours. As the water freezes it expands, and as it does this the shoes will expand and stretch. You will need to allow the shoes to defrost enough to remove the bags of water when you remove them from the freezer.

Cleaning White Canvas Shoes

Apply a paste of automatic dishwashing detergent mixed with hot water to the shoes. Allow to soak at least 30 minutes, then scrub surface with a nail brush or toothbrush. Rinse well and allow to dry. Dry the shoes out of the direct sun. You can also put the shoes in the washing machine with several old white towels and launder as usual after soaking and brushing. To keep the shoes clean, set them on paper and apply several coats of spray starch or fabric protector. They will stay clean longer and soil will wash out more easily.

Cleaning White Leather Athletic Shoes

These can be cleaned easily with whitewall tire cleaner. Take the shoes outside if possible or spray over newspaper. Let sit 2 or 3 minutes and then wipe with paper towels or old rags. Remember, whitewall tire cleaner is a bleaching product, so rinse shoes thoroughly before wearing in the house on carpet. Pay special attention to the soles.

Polishing White Leather

Before polishing, clean well. To remove scuffs, try an art gum eraser or a paste of baking soda and water. To cover scuffs that won't come off, use liquid typewriter correction fluid prior to polishing. Prep the shoes for white polish by rubbing them with the cut side of a raw potato. The potato will help the polish go on smoothly and cover scuff marks.

When You're Out of Shoe Polish

Reach for the furniture polish. Take a rag and spray liberally with furniture polish. Rub the shoe well and buff. In a real hurry, use baby wipes! Rub on and buff.

Fixing Scuffs and Tears on Shoes

If there's a black mark on shoes, try a dab of nail polish remover, rubbing alcohol or lighter fluid on a clean cloth. For areas where the color is removed try using a marker in the same color. Wipe immediately after applying with a paper towel and then polish.

Scuffs on Gold or Silver Shoes

Use an old, dry toothbrush with white toothpaste to remove the scuff; polish with clear polish or furniture polish.

Polishing Patent Leather

Rub petroleum jelly into patent leather and buff with a soft cloth. It not only polishes, it prevents cracking.

Scuff Marks on Vinyl or Plastic Shoes

Use lighter fluid. Be sure to dispose of the rag or paper towel you use outside.

If Plastic Tips Fall Off Your Shoelaces

Easy—twist the ends of the shoelaces and dip in clear nail polish.

To Keep Children's Shoes Tied

Dampen the laces with a spray of water before you tie them. This allows you to tie the bows tighter and the laces will stay in place.

㉙ Turning Down the Heat on Fire Damage

I honestly hope that you never have any reason to do any thing more than just glance through this chapter, but if you ever have a fire in your home, remember it's here. I spent 15 years as the owner of a disaster restoration company in

Michigan and I can tell you that in those first hours after a fire it's all you can do to remember your name.

The fire truck has just left and there you stand amid what once was your home and is now a smelly, wet, black mess that you hardly recognize. You want to sit down and have a good cry, but there isn't any place clean to sit. What do you do now? Is everything ruined? This chapter will help you deal with the emotional turmoil and give you sound information about what you, as the homeowner, need to do.

Just in Case

First, as soon as you are done reading this, put your homeowner's policy, along with your agent's name and phone number, in a fireproof box or bank safety deposit box. This enables you to easily find them and protects them from being destroyed in the fire. Make notes from this chapter and put them with your insurance information.

Get on the Phone

After the fire is out, call your insurance agent or the 800 number that is often provided on your policy to report claims.

Call immediately. It may seem like the damage couldn't be worse, but it could. After a fire there can be ongoing damage from acid soot residue. Fire produces two main pollutants—nitrous oxide (from burning wood, food, etc.) and sulfur dioxide (from burning plastics and petroleum by-products, etc.). When these pollutants combine with moisture and humidity, they form acid! Within hours this can cause substantial and continuing damage. Prompt attention from your local disaster restoration firm will eliminate the problem and prevent further damage to valuables. Disaster restoration companies are listed in your phone directory and are available 24 hours a day for emergencies. They will preserve, protect and secure surfaces that may be subject to continuing damage, and will work with your insurance adjuster to estimate the damage.

What Is an Insurance Adjuster?

The insurance adjuster works for the insurance company. He is an expert in smoke damage, such as chimney fires, furnace backups and actual fire damage. He will help you decide what can be saved and what can't. He will require a written estimate from a disaster restoration company and any contractors or dry cleaners who will participate in the cleanup. Sometimes more than one estimate will be requested.

During this time you will be receiving all kinds of comments and advice from friends, relatives and even strangers. Ignore it! Your insurance adjuster is a professional and knows the best way to handle smoke damage. The adjuster may even be able to give you advice on a company that they have dealt with before if you are unsure who to call.

Disaster Restoration Companies

Disaster restoration companies (i.e. cleaning companies) do two types of cleaning: structural and contents cleaning. Structural cleaning is wall-washing, carpet cleaning, cupboards—the things you can't remove from the house when you move. Contents cleaning is the upholstery, hard furniture, dishes, clothes, etc.—things you take with you when you move. They will provide a complete estimate to the insurance company and a copy to you.

Once coverage is confirmed and appropriate authorizations are secured, the cleaning and repairs will take place as quickly as possible. This will include dry cleaning, laundry and deodorization, also covered in this chapter.

Payment

After completion of all the cleaning and restoration, the insurance company will generally issue a check in your name and in the name of the firm that did the work. Once the work is satisfactory, you sign over the checks.

Deodorization

Deodorization is one of the most important parts of any smoke damage cleanup. Everything smells—even your clothes.

First, the initial odor must be brought under control immediately to make the house habitable, if you are able to live in it during the restoration.

During any reconstruction, exposed interior wall sections will be deodorized and any singed wood will be sealed to prevent odor. In serious fires, deodorization will take place after cleaning, too.

All clothing will have to be deodorized during laundry and dry cleaning, and in serious cases will be put in an ozone room that opens the oxygen molecules and releases odor.

Ozone machines are also used for deodorizing the home, resulting in a smell much like the air after a thunderstorm. The best deodorization technique I have ever known is recreating the conditions causing the odor. In the case of smoke damage a deodorant "smoke" is produced, which allows the deodorization process to penetrate in exactly the same manner the smoke odor did.

Additional odor control is done with duct sealing and deodorization.

Additionally, all walls that are washed and painted should be sealed first with a special sealer to eliminate residue "bleed through" from the oily smoke film. Then the walls are painted in the normal manner. This process is one that your disaster restoration firm and adjuster will be familiar with.

With light smoke damage, many times the wall washing is necessary, but not painting. Deodorization is generally always advised.

What If You Don't Have Insurance?

The best advice I can give you is to carry insurance. If you live in an apartment or condominium, buy renter's insurance. If smoke damage occurs, you'll be glad you did.

But, if you don't have insurance, here's some helpful advice:

Go to a janitorial supply store and ask their advice on which cleaning chemicals to use. They can provide you with a professional-quality deodorant to wash clothes, linens and hard surfaces. You will put this deodorant in the water that you clean with or wash clothes with.

Call a disaster restoration firm and try to rent an ozone machine to deodorize the structure and your contents, bearing in mind that prolonged ozone use will yellow plastics. Buy a soot and dirt removal sponge to clean walls. This is somewhat like a blackboard eraser that removes oily smoke film, so that when you begin to wash the walls the sooty film won't smear.

Rent a carpet cleaning machine with an upholstery attachment to clean carpet and all upholstery that can be cleaned with water.

Wash hard furniture with oil soap and dry, then use furniture polish if you want a brighter shine.

Wash Everything

Wash everything thoroughly—this means walls, cupboards, collectibles, dishes, clothes, etc., otherwise the odor will remain.

Start in one room and do it completely except for carpet cleaning (you'll track during the cleaning process and spread soot on the carpet). Clean the carpet in all rooms last.

If you still have odor, do a final deodorization with an ozone machine, or if you can, hire a firm to come in and do it for you.

The Big Drip—
Water Damage
Restoration

What a shock! When you left the house everything was fine.

You come home and unlock the door; you walk in and hear the sound of running water. As you step in, water comes up to your ankles. Now you find water running across the carpet and floors and lapping at the legs of furniture as the sofa and chairs try to soak it up. Here's what you need to do immediately.

Turn It Off

First, know where your water shut-off is and use it. Turn off the water and look for the source of the leak. BE SURE THE ELECTRICAL POWER SOURCE IS OFF BEFORE YOU WALK IN STANDING WATER. The leak could be from a toilet, the washing machine hoses, or a broken pipe.

How quickly you react will have impact on what can be saved in your home.

Call the Professionals

Now that you have shut off the water and located the problem, call your insurance agent. Your agent will act quickly to help you, because by the time an adjuster receives the information it is often too late to reverse some of the damage that has taken place.

Wet carpet and pad are restorable if it is taken care of as soon as possible after the damage has occurred.

A professional company that deals in water damage of all kinds can stop further damage from occurring and also save the carpet and pad.

To find a water damage expert, look in the yellow pages under "water damage" or under "cleaning companies" or "disaster restoration firms." Be sure to get a company that specializes in this problem.

Dry Out

First they will extract water from the pad and the carpet and treat both with an EPA-registered disinfectant. They will then install drying equipment, which consists of high-powered carpet blowers that are slipped between the carpet and the pad. They also will install dehumidification equipment to facilitate drying. They will advise you to keep your home's interior temperature at 70 degrees or warmer for ideal drying conditions. This drying equipment will also facilitate drying of upholstered furniture and walls as it dries the carpet.

Upholstered furniture will need to have water extracted from it and be treated with an EPA-registered disinfectant, too. Wood furniture will be wiped down and allowed to dry.

The water damage restoration firm will check, usually every 24 hours, to see how the drying process is coming and to move equipment to continue the drying process.

What Is an Antimicrobial?

Many water damage restoration firms have a wonderful antimicrobial product available that not only disinfects, but also inhibits the growth of mold, mildew and bacterial

spores. This is applied to the carpet after extraction takes place and has certainly saved many a carpet.

After all the carpet and contents of your home are dry, the upholstery and carpet will be cleaned and again treated with a disinfectant product or antimicrobial. Hard furniture will be washed and polished and hard floors will be given a final cleaning. If your carpet or upholstery had a protective coating on it, this will be reapplied.

Walls will be washed as needed and your home will be returned to normal once again.

Answers to Your Sea of Worries

The Pad Will Dissolve!

Not so! Most pads are made of nonwater-sensitive foam bonded with a dry solvent-soluble adhesive.

The Seams Will Separate!

Now that is logical. Wet carpet naturally means shrinkage, right? WRONG! Nonwater-soluble adhesives are used on seams. Regardless of what happens, seams can be repaired.

The Carpet Shrank Off the Wall!

Only poorly installed carpet will come loose from the wall and this is easily restretched.

The Carpet Will Fall Apart!

This is not likely. During the manufacturing process carpet manufacturers actually immerse carpet in water many times during the dyeing and rinsing process. Synthetic fibers, the primary backings, and latex adhesives are virtually unaffected by water for at least 48 hours.

Sewer Backups

If your water damage is due to a sewer backup, these restoration firms are trained to deal with it. Stay out of the water and waste. Let the trained experts deal with the water and bacterial problems; that's their job and they know what can be saved and what can't.

31

Taking the Atchoo-Cough-Cough Out of Your Air Ducts

Picture yourself in this situation: You have had smoke damage in your home. All the cleaning and repainting is done and now you are ready to turn on the furnace. You go to the thermostat and turn it up. You hear the furnace spring to life. The central blower is activated . . . and, suddenly, you run screaming from the house. What's wrong? All the odor that collected in the duct system during the smoke damage has just been blown full force from the duct system and into the house. It smells like the house is on fire again. As if the smell isn't enough, you now see black soot residue blowing out in a dark cloud and settling all over the newly cleaned walls, carpet and furniture. How could this happen? Nobody thought to clean the duct system prior to cleaning the house and turning on the furnace.

Duct cleaning and deodorizing is not just for houses that have had fire or smoke damage. It is very beneficial in older homes where dust and allergy-causing bacteria have accumulated in the duct work and are blown through the home each time the furnace runs. Duct cleaning can be very beneficial for people who have allergy problems, too.

What Is Duct Cleaning?

Duct cleaning consists of removing register covers and vacuuming out all the duct work that leads to the furnace. After some elaborate preparatory vacuuming and cleaning procedures, which include cleaning all the register covers, a duct sealer is introduced into the system in the form of a fine mist. This sealer is a plastic-like resin. The chemical itself actually neutralizes odor and seals onto the interior walls of the system the loose soot, dust and dirt that remain after vacuuming. During this process all odor is eliminated and minor residues remaining in unseen or unreachable areas are permanently sealed onto the interior surface of the ducts.

This process gives you a dirt-, dust- and pollen-free environment. If allergies run in your family you will immediately notice the difference. This is particularly good in older homes that, naturally, have the original duct systems in place.

When you have this procedure done it is a good idea to have your furnace cleaned at the same time. Many furnace companies clean duct work, too, as do many disaster restoration or cleaning companies.

Fresh Air

You've had smoke damage . . . you have allergies . . . you just purchased an older home. . . . This is some healthy advice for cleaner air and a fresher smell.

32

Stop the Science Experiment— Mold and Mildew

Left unchecked, dampness in a home or basement can rot wood, peel paint and promote rust and mildew.

Find the Source

Here is a simple test to determine if dampness is caused by seepage or excessive humidity:

Cut several 12-inch squares of aluminum foil. Tape them

in various spots on the floor and walls; seal the edges tightly. If moisture collects between the foil and the surface after several days, waterproof the interior walls. If moisture forms on the foil's surface, take the following steps:

Close windows on humid days.

Install a window exhaust fan.

Vent your clothes dryer to the outside.

Use a dehumidifier, especially during summer months.

Treat walls with epoxy-based waterproofing paint or masonry sealer. (To clean walls in preparation for paint, look for special mildew cleaners in home centers.)

Make Your Own Treatment

You can also make your own mildew treatment by mixing a quart of chlorine bleach and a tablespoon of powdered non-ammoniated laundry detergent with 3 quarts of warm water. Scrub the mildew-stained surface with the solution and allow it to work until the discoloration vanishes, rinse thoroughly and allow to dry.

Caution

Be sure to wear goggles, rubber gloves and protective clothing when using this solution. Never allow it to come in contact with carpet or fabrics, and clean the shoes you wear before walking on carpets. Do this in a well-ventilated area.

Resource Guide

ACT NATURAL CLOTHS™: See Euronet USA.

ART GUM ERASER: You remember the little brownish-tan rectangular eraser that you used in school, the one that crumbled as you erased? That's the one!

BAKING POWDER: If you bake, you already have this in the cupboard. If not, look in the baking section near the baking soda. Baking powder and baking soda are not the same thing, so don't even go there!

BEESWAX: Is usually found in drugstores, hardware stores and natural product stores. If you don't see it, ask!

BITTER APPLE: This keeps pets from dining on your plants, etc. It is not harmful to them, but tastes terrible so it discourages them entirely. Look for it at pet supply stores.

BORAX: Better known as Twenty Mule Team Borax, this laundry additive can be found in the detergent aisle.

BRUCE FLOOR CARE PRODUCTS: Look for these

products at hardware stores, home centers and wherever wood flooring is sold.

CALGON WATER SOFTENER®: Look for it with the laundry additives at the grocery store.

CHAMOIS: Found in hardware stores and home centers.

CHARCOAL: This is the type made for fish tanks and is available at pet supply stores.

CLEAR AMMONIA: There are two types of ammonia, clear and sudsy. Clear contains no soap and should be used where suggested for that reason.

COLD CREAM: Plain old Ponds that your grandma used on her face, or the store brand.

CUTICLE REMOVER: The gel you apply to your cuticles to soften them. Let's be clear, it is cuticle remover, NOT nail polish remover.

DENATURED ALCOHOL: This is an industrial alcohol reserved for heavy-duty cleaning. Don't use it near open flame and dispose of any rags that were used to apply it outside the home. Launder or clean anything that you treat with it as soon as possible. Look for this in cans at hardware stores and home centers. Remember the Queen's rule: always test in an inconspicuous place before treating a large area with this product.

ENERGINE CLEANING FLUID®: Look for this at the hardware store, the home center and even in some grocery stores (usually on the top shelf with the laundry additives).

EURONET USA: Makers of the Act Natural™ microfiber cloths and mops. They clean and disinfect without chemicals using only water. They have been scientifically proven to kill germs and bacteria and even come with a warranty. They are easy to use, great for people with allergies, and can be cleaned and sanitized in the washer (this is particularly important with the mop). Use them in the kitchen, bathroom, to spot carpet, on windows, mirrors, hard furniture, in the car, virtually anywhere you clean. Call 888-638 2882 or visit www.euronetusa.com. They are a wonderful invest ment. My mop is almost two years old and is still doing the job.

FELS-NAPTHA SOAP®: What a wonderful laundry spotter and cleaner this is. You'll find it in the bar soap section of the grocery store. It's usually on the bottom shelf in a small stack and always has dust on it, because nobody knows what to use it for.

FINE DRYWALL SANDPAPER: This sandpaper looks like window screen. Make sure you buy a package marked "fine grade."

FINE STEEL WOOL: Look for the symbol "0000" and the word FINE. And don't try soap-filled steel wool pads. They are not acceptable substitutes.

GLYCERIN: Look for glycerin in drugstores in the hand cream section. Always purchase plain glycerin, not the type containing rosewater.

GO-JO WATERLESS HAND CLEANER®: People with greasy hands have used this product for years. It's a hand cleaner and so much more. Look for it at home centers and hardware stores.

HYDROGEN PEROXIDE: Choose the type that you use on cuts and to gargle with—not the type used to bleach hair. That will remove color from carpet or fabric.

INVISIBLE SHIELD® SURFACE TREATMENT: This is such a wonderful product that just the name gives me goose bumps! It turns all of those hard to clean surfaces in your home (tub, shower, shower doors, sinks, counters, stovetops, windows, any surface that is not wood or painted) into nonstick surfaces that can be cleaned with water and a soft cloth. No more soap scum or hard-water deposits! It never builds up on surfaces so it won't make them slippery, and it's nontoxic, so you can use it on dishes and food surfaces too. Call 800-528-3149 to find a supplier near you.

LEMON OR ORANGE EXTRACT: These are found in the spice area of the grocery store where vanilla extract is sold.

LINSEED OIL: You'll find this at the hardware store, usually in the paint and staining section. It is combustible, so use care in disposing of rags or paper towels used to apply it. Keep it in the garage or basement away from open flame.

MEAT TENDERIZER: Use the unseasoned variety please, or you will have a whole new stain to deal with. Store brands work fine.

NAIL POLISH REMOVER: I caution you to use nonacetone polish remover, which is much less aggressive than acetone polish remover. (Straight acetone is exceedingly strong.) Use only where recommended and with great care. Look for this product at beauty supply stores.

NATURAL SPONGE: A natural sponge is the best sponge you will ever use. It has hundreds of natural "scrubbing fingers" that make any wall-washing job speed by. Look for these at home centers and hardware stores and choose a nice size to fit your hand. Wash them in lukewarm water with gentle suds. You can put them in the washing machine if you avoid combining them with fabrics that have lint.

NATURE'S MIRACLE®: An enzyme-based odor removal product for urine-based pet accidents. Available at pet supply stores across the country.

NON-GEL TOOTHPASTE: This is just a fancy name for old-fashioned plain white toothpaste. Gels just don't work, so don't even try.

ODORZOUT®: A fabulous, dry, 100 percent natural deodorizer. It's nontoxic, so you can use it any place you have a smell or a stink. It is especially effective on pet urine odors, and since it is used dry it is simple to apply. Call 800-88STINK, or visit their website at www.88stink.com.

OIL OF CLOVES: Widely available at health food stores, vitamin stores and natural food stores.

OUTRIGHT PET ODOR ELIMINATOR®: An enzyme odor removal product for urine-based pet accidents. Available at pet supply stores across the country.

POWDERED ALUM: This old-fashioned product was once used in pickling. Look for it at drugstores and if you can't find it, ask the pharmacist.

ROTTENSTONE: Mild pumice, look for it at hardware stores and home centers.

RUST REMOVER: These are serious products so follow the directions carefully. Look for products like Whink® and Rust Magic® at hardware stores and home centers.

SADDLE SOAP: You will find this in the hardware store, or in the shoe polish section at most any store.

SHAVING CREAM: The cheaper brands work fine and shaving cream works better than gel.

SOAPWORKS: Manufacturer of wonderful nontoxic, user- and earth-friendly cleaning, laundry and personal care products. Try their At Home All-Purpose Cleaner™, originally designed for allergy and asthma sufferers. Soapworks products are very effective, and they are economical, so everyone can use them. Call 800-699-9917 or visit their website at www.soapworks.com.

SOOT AND DIRT REMOVAL SPONGE: These are used to clean walls, wallpaper, lampshades and even soot. They also remove pet hair from upholstery. These big brick erasers are available at home centers and hardware stores, usually near the wallpaper supplies. Clean them by washing in a pail of warm water and liquid dish soap, rinse well and allow to dry before using again.

SPOT SHOT INSTANT CARPET STAIN REMOVER®: My all-time favorite carpet spotter and I have tried them all! Try SPOT SHOT UPHOLSTERY STAIN REMOVER® too. Available most everywhere, or call 800-848-4389.

SQUEEGEE: When buying a squeegee for washing windows, look for a good quality one with a replaceable rubber blade. Always be sure that the rubber blade is soft and flexible for best results. Look for these at hardware stores, home centers and janitorial supply companies. They come in different widths, so be sure to think about the size windows, etc., that you are going to use it for. A 12-inch blade is a good starting point.

TACK-TRAP®: Bugs are drawn to the color of this sticky sheet. Sold in garden supply stores and some hardware stores.

TANG™ BREAKFAST DRINK: Yes, this is the product that the astronauts took to the moon! It is also a great cleaner. (Store brands work just as well.)

TRISODIUM PHOSPHATE (TSP): Cleaning professionals have used this product for years. It is wonderful for washing walls, garage floors and any tough cleaning job. Look for it at hardware stores, home centers and janitorial supply stores. Wear rubber gloves when using it.

TYPEWRITER ERASER: A thing of the past, but still available at office supply stores. Shaped like a pencil with a little brush where the pencil eraser would be, they can be sharpened like a pencil and will last for years.

WASHING SODA: I like Arm & Hammer™ Washing Soda, which can be found in the detergent aisle at the grocery store along with other laundry additives. No, you can not substitute baking soda, it is a different product!

WAX CRAYONS: These are sold in hardware stores and home centers and come in various wood colors for concealing scratches in wood surfaces. Don't be fooled by the color name; try to take along a sample of what you need to patch to get the best possible match.

WD-40™ LUBRICANT: I bet you will find a can in your garage or basement. Fine spray oil for lubricating all kinds of things, it's a wonderful product for regenerating grease so that it can be removed from clothes. Look for WD-40™ at the hardware store, home center and even the grocery store.

WHITING: Look for this at the hardware store, usually near the paint.

WINDOW SCRUBBER: This looks like a squeegee wearing a coat. Look for it at janitorial supply stores and home centers.

WINE AWAY RED WINE STAIN REMOVER™: This unbelievable product can remove red stains, such as red wine, red pop, cranberry juice, red food coloring, grape juice, etc., from carpet and fabric. It is totally nontoxic and made from fruit and vegetable extracts. I just can't believe how well it works! Look for it where liquor is sold or call 888-WINE-AWAY for a store location near you.

WINTERGREEN OIL: Widely available at health food stores, natural food stores and some linen stores.

ZUD HEAVY DUTY CLEANSER®: This is a wonderful cleanser for really tough jobs. It works great on rust on hard surfaces too. Find it at hardware stores, home centers and grocery stores. Well worth keeping on hand.

Index

Talking
Dirty Laundry
with the
Queen of Clean®

My grateful thanks to:

My husband John, The King. Without you there would be no reason for my heart to sing, no reason to smile, no reason to laugh, and nothing to talk dirty about.

Dad, your loving smile, your gentle face, no one can fill your vacant place.

The Queen Mom. Without you there would be no Queen of Clean. Thanks for always being proud of me no matter what I did.

David and Janette; Victoria; Pat, Laura, John and Justin; Nancy and Drew; Nanette, David and Patrick, our wonderful, loving combined family. They aren't just our kids and grandchildren, they are our friends.

Betty Archambeau, who is always there with a smile and a hug.

Peggy Barker, who proves to me daily that age *is* only a state of mind.

Brenda Copeland, my editor. I think we share brain cells we are so in tune with each other. Thank you, Brenda, for your moral support, laughter, your warm heart, and your dirty cleaning questions!

Beth Deveny, your moral support and hard work have been priceless.

Chuck Soderstrom, Duane Dooling, and everyone at Anderson News. Thank you for your belief in the Queen and the incredible launch you gave Talking Dirty.

Win and Carolyn Holden. Without you I would not be "Talking Dirty!"

Alan Centofante. You never run out of ideas or the ability to present them.

Jana Bommersbach. You are an inspiration and the yardstick I measure myself by.

Preston and Eleanor Coon. You have been the kindest, most faithful friends anyone could ever have, through the good and not so good.

All of you who continue to "talk dirty to me!" Because of you it really *is* good to be Queen!

Contents

Contents

Foreword

Did your mom ever tell you, "don't air your dirty laundry in public," and "always wear clean underwear just in case you are in an accident"? The Queen Mother said it to me when I was growing up. Back then I wasn't sure what she meant. Now I think it sounds like a great lead into a laundry book!

You *can* air your dirty laundry with me—and so can your mother. In fact, I hope you will, because I'm the Queen of Clean® and I'm going to show you ways you've never thought of to keep your underwear clean . . . and everything else too!

If you are "laundry challenged" you have come to the right place. This is where you'll find laundry basics such as how to care for your washer and dryer; how to choose a detergent and softener; and how to make inexpensive and effective laundry stain removers. I'm going to talk about some great laundry products, and introduce you to some of the great stain-fighting ingredients you already have in your cupboard. I'm going to give you the lowdown on ironing and dry cleaning, and I'm even going to tell you how to care for bedspreads, slipcovers, and lampshades!

You're in good hands. So sit back, prop your feet up on that clothes hamper, and let's talk dirty . . . laundry, that is!

—Linda Cobb

P.S. If you have any laundry or cleaning problems you'd like me to address in my next book, just drop me a line at:

Queen of Clean® Suggestion Box
PO Box 655
Peoria, AZ 85380

And don't forget to visit my website, queenofclean.com

Part I

·····················

THE BASICS

1
Care and Control of the Washing Machine

How difficult can it be? You add water and detergent, drop in the clothes, select the cycle and walk away. When you come back the clothes are clean. Okay . . . but have you ever considered how clean your washing machine is after all that hard water and *all* those dirty clothes?

Your washer needs some TLC from time to time, especially if you have hard water in your area. So if the clothes seem dull and gray, maybe you don't need that new and improved detergent. Maybe all you need to do is clean the washing machine. Here's the easiest way I know.

Fill the washer with hot water. Add 1 quart of chlorine

bleach (no detergent, please). Run the washer through the longest wash cycle. When the washer is still wet—this should be immediately after the bleach cycle—add 1 quart of white vinegar and run the washer through the same cycle again. This will clean out soap scum and mineral deposits from the spin basket and also from the hoses. If you live in an area with hard water you really need to do this every three months—otherwise, every six months will do. You'll be amazed at the difference it will make.

If you start to notice little brown, rusty-looking spots on clothes when they come out of the washing machine, well, it probably *is* rust! Look your spin basket over carefully when this occurs, and check for any chips in the finish. Chipped areas rust and transfer to clothes, and the only way to remedy this problem is to replace the spin basket. Check with your appliance dealer and be sure to get the right basket for your machine. And a word of caution: Take care when using detergent balls or fabric softener balls. They can chip the spin basket with their weight.

For information on removing rust stains from clothes, turn to the spotting section. It's easier than you think.

Quick Clean Method

When you don't have time to give your machine a really thorough clean, just fill the washer with hot water and pour in 1 gallon of white vinegar. Run through the entire wash cycle.

Cleaning the Fabric Softener Dispenser

Clean the automatic fabric softener dispenser every month to 6 weeks to keep it working well and to prevent it from leaving softener stains on clothes. (Liquid softener can leave blue spots on clothes; marks from dryer sheets can look like small grease patches.) To clean the dispenser you first must warm 1 cup of white vinegar (I use the microwave), and pour it into the dispenser as you would softener. Make sure you use warm vinegar, and make sure you do this when the washer is empty. Large pieces of sticky fabric softener will occasionally be flushed out during cleaning, and they could adhere to clothes. Not a pretty sight. I suggest cleaning the fabric softener dispenser when you are cleaning the machine with one of the methods recommended in this chapter.

Cleaning the Bleach Dispenser

It is equally important to keep the bleach dispenser clean. Clean any removable parts by washing with hot water and dishwashing liquid. When you clean the washer with white vinegar, be sure to add some to the bleach dispenser too.

QUICK TIP

Use less detergent and you will have less soap buildup on clothes *and* in the washing machine. Use ½ cup of Arm and Hammer Washing Soda™ and about half the amount of detergent you would usually use. Adjust this formula by increasing or decreasing detergent per your individual needs.

Tips on Buying and Placing a New Washing Machine

If you don't have space for a washer and dryer to sit next to each other, remember that you can buy some very efficient stackable units. Just make sure to measure the area *before* you buy.

A front-loading washer is definitely a space saver—the top makes a great work space for spotting clothes. You'll need to protect the top of the washer if you are going to work off it, though. A plastic breadboard is ideal.

Another good feature of front-loading washers is the way they tumble clothes. They generally tumble clothes the way a dryer does, and that's gentler on fabric than agitating. It is also less wobbly when spinning. The downside is that front-loaders generally have a smaller capacity than top-loaders, and they're usually not as good at cleaning heavy, ground-in dirt.

There are many top loaders to choose from. Consider your needs carefully. You may want an extra-large capacity washer if you wash large loads of towels and sheets, but do make sure you don't overbuy. It's a waste of money to buy bells and whistles you don't need—and there's more to go wrong, too!

Give your washing machine plenty of room to vibrate. Allow an inch of space all the way around the machine.

To keep the exterior of your washer and dryer clean and shiny, make sure you apply a coat of Clean Shield® (formerly Invisible Shield®) as soon as you buy your machine. This will put an invisible nonstick finish on the surface that will keep it looking like new. Water will bead up and wipe off, as will detergent and spotters. Re-apply as needed.

Important: If your washer's power cord does not reach the outlet, have the outlet moved or the power cord replaced with a longer one. Absolutely never use an extension cord between the washer's power cord and the outlet. If water touches the connection between the extension cord and the power cord, you could be electrocuted.

Do not install your washer in an unheated garage or utility room. Water that is trapped inside can freeze and severely damage the machine.

One last installation tip: If you are installing a washing machine in a vacation home that is not heated during cold weather, have it drained completely by an appliance service technician before shutting up the home for the winter. Again, trapped water can freeze and damage the machine.

If I can leave you with a final piece of advice concerning washing machines it would be this: NEVER leave home when the washing machine is running. It only takes seconds for a hose to break or a malfunction to occur and that can cause damage and flooding in your home. I cannot tell you how many water damage cleanups we did when I owned my cleaning and disaster restoration company in Michigan. The amount of water that can pour from a small hose is unbelievable. So is the damage that can be done—not only to things that can be cleaned or replaced but also to precious treasures that can never be saved. It's heartbreaking.

2

Drying: How to Succeed Without Really Trying

Now we have the clothes washed and ready for the dryer, so let's talk dirty dryers!

Keeping the dryer clean is important: A clean dryer will work more efficiently, saving you time and money. A clean dryer will also help to prevent dryer fires. Dryer fires are much more common than you might think, so avoid them at all costs.

First the basics:

If you have a lint-clogged dryer venting system, your clothes will not dry properly and you will waste time and money running longer cycles to get the clothes completely dry. Turn the dryer on, and go outside and hold your hand under the dryer vent hood—you know, that metal thing on the outside of the house. If you don't feel a strong flow of air it's time to clean. Clean the dryer vent pipe or flex exhaust hose once a year to prevent lint buildup. Try to lock a date in your mind and do it every year. I like Halloween 'cause you can extract the lint and create a dust bunny costume at the same time! Remove the duct or hose from the dryer back and the exhaust mounting, and shake it out. It may be necessary to run an old cloth through the hose to dislodge any lint that is unwilling or unable to leave the vent. Be sure to reseal the joints, using a fresh piece of duct tape if necessary.

While you have the dryer out, vacuum and wash the floor area underneath the unit. If you see any grease or oil leaks on the floor, it's time to call the appliance repairman.

On the outside of the vent, clean the hood and vent by using a straightened wire coat hanger or bottle-type brush. Push it back and forth in the vent to remove accumulated lint.

Always make sure that your vent is straight. Kinks will block the airflow.

The lint filter in the dryer is no less important than the vent. Keeping it clean is vital. A clogged lint filter allows lint to accumulate and can eventually start a fire. A dirty lint filter also blocks airflow, so your clothes will take longer to dry. And that means extra money on your gas or electric bill.

To clean the filter, remove it, wipe off the lint and replace. You can do this easily by wiping the filter with a used dryer fabric softener sheet, which will collect the accumulated lint so that you can dispose of it without additional mess.

It's important to vacuum the filter periodically, and to clean the area where the lint filter is installed with vacuum attachments. (This is the opening on the dryer that the filter slides into.)

Important: If you have a gas dryer, always use caution not to kink or damage the gas line when shifting.

Dryer Dilemmas

Now that you know how to clean the dryer, it's time to talk about some quick, easy tips to make your job a lot easier. Anyone who does laundry knows how those little OOPS! can happen and how frustrating they can be. So let's de-oops the clothes dryer!

Lint-Free Drying

If you're drying clothes that have lint—or a big oops, a tissue has gone through the washer—put a piece of nylon net in the dryer along with the clothes. The net will catch the lint effectively so you won't have to drag out the lint roller, or worse still, pick off all of the fuzz. I buy cheap nylon net from a fabric store and throw it out when it's full of lint.

Oops! I Forgot to Take the Clothes Out of the Dryer

We all know that if you take items out of the dryer as soon as it shuts off, you can fold or hang your clothes with little or no ironing. But you can't always get to the dryer immediately. Let's be honest. How many times have you gone to the dryer and found a load of clothes that were forgotten? Oops! The clothes are a mass of wrinkles! Don't go to the trouble of rewashing the clothes, and don't iron them, either. Just toss a damp towel in the dryer and rerun the load for a few minutes. The wrinkles will release and you can hang up the clothes. Remember, though, never use a white towel with dark clothes or you will give yourself another problem . . . lint!

Yikes! How Did That Get in the Dryer?

To remove crayon, lipstick or Chap Stick® from the dryer, turn it off and spray a paper towel with WD-40 Lubricant®. Wipe out the dryer until all of the mess is removed. Wash out with warm water and dishwashing liquid, then dry a load of old wet rags.

Try Carbona® Stain Devils to remove chewing gum and glue. For ink, use rubbing alcohol or Ink Away™ by the makers of Goo Gone™.

Don't Even Think of Putting That in the Dryer!

Don't put stained or spotted clothes in the dryer. The heat will set the stain, making it next to impossible to remove. Re-treat the stain with one of the appropriate methods mentioned in this book, and launder again.

Important: Do not put anything in the dryer that has come in contact with paint, gasoline, oil used on machinery, etc., or any flammable fluids. These things are fire hazards and the fumes they give off can ignite. If they come in contact with a hot dryer you could have a serious problem. Line dry these items.

DRYER QUICK TIPS

- Clean the dryer lint filter after each use.

- Always check to see that the dryer is empty before using.

- Avoid drying extremely small loads or crowding the dryer with extra large loads. Very small loads can clump, and very large loads don't tumble well. Both waste time and energy.

- Dry lightweight fabrics together and heavy fabrics together for more efficient drying.

- Dry loads one after another. That way you can utilize the heat already in the dryer.

- Don't add wet clothes to clothes that are almost dry. This wastes energy—and money!

3

Getting the Hang of Line Drying

We have come full circle. For years it seemed like the dryer had taken over and that clotheslines were obsolete. Now, we are returning to the days of natural fabrics, with drip-dry clothes, clothes that need to be laid flat to dry, and clothes that cannot be put in the dryer for any reason. Don't worry. You don't need a clothesline in the backyard to care for some of these hang-to-dry clothes.

The Basics

As your grandma will tell you, don't spin out too much water from clothes that you are going to hang to dry: that sets in the wrinkles. Instead, shut off the washer halfway through the spin cycle and hang the clothes on a clothesline, allowing for plenty of air circulation between clothes. Dry colored clothes out of direct sunlight (the sun fades them), but hang white clothes in the sun—this will bleach them to an incredible, eye-popping white. They'll smell great too.

Hanging clothes on plastic hangers with sloped ends will allow them to dry without those awful "shoulder dimples." You'll avoid rust that way too!

Specific Drying Tips

Trousers: Hang these by the cuffs. The weight of the trousers will usually keep the legs wrinkle-free, which means less or no pressing. We like that!

Sweaters: To prevent sweaters from having "shoulder dimples" or "clothespin points," thread the legs of an old pair of panty hose through the arms of the sweater, and pull the waist out through the neck. Attach clothespins to the feet and waist of the panty hose instead of the sweater. Just make sure to remove the panty hose before you put on the sweater. Unless you plan to rob a bank . . .

Dresses and coats: When hanging heavy dresses and coats to dry, use two hangers to absorb the weight. If hanging them outside to dry, hook the two hangers in the opposite direction to keep the breeze from blowing the garment off the line.

Lingerie and panty hose: These are better dried in the house over the shower bar, on a small bathroom clothesline, or from plastic hangers with clips.

Handy Hints

• If you do use a clothesline outside, remember to keep it clean by washing it periodically.

• Strong sun will eventually weaken fibers, so keep an eye on the clothes and bring them in as soon as they are dry.

• Bedding washed and hung out to dry occasionally will be crisp and fresh-smelling. White linens will be brighter!

• Do not air-dry down comforters. They dry too slowly and mold or mildew may form in the process.

• A tension curtain rod hung in a laundry room makes a great place to hang clothes to dry. A piece of chain also works well, and you can hook hangers through the links.

• If a garment label says "hang to dry," don't put it in the dryer. It may shrink, or the fibers may distort.

• If clothes are wrinkled after line drying, putting them in the dryer on the "no heat" or "air fluff" setting may save you from ironing them. (Do not use a fabric softener sheet, though. Without heat, fabric softener sheets can stain clothes.)

4

Laundry Detergents and Great Alternatives

I don't think there is a greater laundry challenge than walking down the soap and detergent aisle and deciding what products to buy. We are constantly bombarded with ads about how well this one cleans, how well that one smells . . . this one contains bleach, that one contains optic brighteners, and that one over there . . . well, it contains every cleaning agent known to man—and woman. Argh! But what really matters in a laundry detergent? When is more just too much?

I have a rule that I follow with laundry detergent, and it's this: less is more. When I want a laundry detergent or soap I want that and only that. Period. I want to be the one who determines when I need bleach, softener, or other additives, so I opt for the simplest product that basically does one thing: removes and suspends soil from my clothes and leaves them clean and fresh. Now by *fresh,* I don't mean have a smelly odor after the wash. I like to leave the house without advertising what detergent I use by the way I smell. I like the labels that read "FREE." I don't want odor or artificial color, just the cleaning product. It is healthier for the body and the clothes. If I want to have a fragrance, I will choose the perfume. I don't want to smell like combinations of soap and softener and other laundry products all mixed together.

Basic laundry detergent: This is where it all starts. Choose your laundry product (bear in mind my lecture above), and measure it into the machine. Remember to adjust the amount of detergent used to the size of your load. (You may need to adjust the amount if you have hard water.) More is not better where laundry soap is concerned. It's just harder to rinse out. Detergent residue makes fabric sticky, and that makes it attract soil faster.

What laundry detergent do I use? I've tested them all, and believe me, that was a challenge. Sometimes the detergent that gets out the most spills and spots is not the one that is best for your clothes, or your family. Some laundry detergents are particularly hard on colored fabrics, fading them and giving dark colors a whitish cast.

After more testing than you can imagine, I have picked one detergent that I believe can be all things to all people: PUREX®. It is gentle on clothes and gentle on you, and available in enough varieties so that you can decide whether you want additives and fragrance, etc. It is gentle on colors, tough on whites, and with the addition of Twenty Mule Team Borax®, can remove the very worst messes. For general laundry, just follow the directions on the box or bottle. I am a liquid soap kind of Queen, because I like to measure out my detergent in the cap, and then do a little pre-spotting with it before I toss the clothes and the balance of the detergent in the machine.

Laundry additives: If you have a particularly soiled load of clothes and feel that your detergent needs a kick, try a safe additive like Twenty Mule Team Borax® Laundry Booster. This will help detergent work better without bleach. It removes soils and stains, brightens clothes, and freshens laundry without an artificial smell. It's been around since 1891, so it's definitely passed that test of time! Use about ½ cup per wash load when you need that extra cleaning power for things such as work clothes, towels, rugs, etc.

Twenty Mule Team Borax® is great for diapers. It's completely safe for baby clothes and hand washables. It's also a great deodorizer and has more uses in cleaning than I can name.

Allergy-free products: Many people, particularly children, have allergies and asthma problems which seem to be directly related to the cleaning and laundry products we use in our homes. If your family appears to be allergic to its underwear (no, I'm not kidding), it may be your detergent. I've been researching allergy-free, nontoxic cleaning products for a long time, and I'm happy to tell you that I have found environmentally friendly products that work to avoid these reactions.

I've tested these products. They work safely on laundry for the whole family, babies to adults.

The following products are made by a company called Soapworks. They were created by a woman in direct response to her son's severe, life-threatening asthma. Try the Fresh Breeze Laundry Powder™ or the Fresh Breeze Liquid™. It is made from natural ingredients such as coconut and palm kernel soap. This can be used to safely spot clothes and presoak too, and has a light, fresh scent of natural ginger. Cost for the powder soap works out to about 5 cents per load compared with about 18 cents a load for a reasonably priced detergent.

They also make Sun Shine Liquid Soap™ for dishes and washing delicates, and again, it is all natural.

In Chapter 8, I'll tell you about Soapworks Brilliant Bleach™, which is a hydrogen peroxide-based bleach.

There is something for everyone in the laundry aisle, but a word of caution: not all clothes require those heavy-duty products. They can be hard on fabrics and on the environment. Grandma didn't need those additives, and her clothes lasted a long time.

5

Be a Spot
Hot Shot!

I love natural products, and I love things that I can make for pennies and still have them work better than the products I could buy at the store. Here are some of my favorite laundry spot removers. Use them just as you would over-the-counter products, but take note: many of them are designed to take care of specific spots and stains.

Start with a clean spray and/or squeeze bottle, and always be sure to label any product you make. It's important to know what the bottle contains and what it was intended for. I like to include the recipe on the label too—that way I can mix up additional product with ease. Cover the label with clear packaging tape or a piece of clear adhesive sheet to protect the label from moisture.

These spotters are all intended for washable fabrics. If in doubt, test in an inconspicuous spot, such as a seam.

General All-Purpose Laundry Spotter

Combine the following to make a generic spotter that works on a wide variety of stains:

1 part rubbing alcohol

2 parts water

If you use a large spray bottle you can add 1 bottle of alcohol and 2 of the alcohol bottles filled with water. Spray this on spots and spills, wait a few minutes, and then launder as usual.

Beverage, Fruit and Grass Remover

Combine equal portions of:

white vinegar

liquid dishwashing soap

water

Shake well and work the solution into the spot. Let stand a few minutes and then launder as usual.

Non-oily Stain Remover

Combine equal portions of the following ingredients:

ammonia

liquid dishwashing soap

water

Shake well, and work the solution into the spot. Let stand a few minutes and flush with water. This solution works well on stains such as milk, blood, perspiration and urine. *Do not use on washable wool, silk, spandex, acrylic and acetate.*

Oily Stain Remover
Combine the following:
    1 tablespoon glycerin
    1 tablespoon liquid dishwashing soap
    8 tablespoons of water
Work the solution into grease and oil stains. Let sit a few minutes, flush with water and launder as usual.

Again, remember all of these spotters are for washable fabrics only and none of them are for silk, wool, spandex, acrylic and acetate. When in doubt, test first!

6
Bringing Out the Big Guns

It's time to talk about the big guns of laundry spotters. We all need them from time to time. But what's best? What really works? Read on. I've tried them all, so you won't have to!

A quick disclaimer: Remember, I am counting on you to test a small, inconspicuous area on the fabric for colorfastness *before* you use any of these spotters. Don't let laundry spotters dry. Launder soon after spotting to prevent the spot from becoming a stain. Don't let me down!

Energine Cleaning Fluid®: This is a terrific "can't be without" spotter for dry-clean-only clothes. Blot it on until the stain is gone and then blow-dry to avoid a ring.

Fels-Naptha Heavy Duty Laundry Bar Soap®: This is that old-fashioned brown bar soap that your grandmother used. It has been around 100 years—literally!—and it's a great spotter for numerous spots and stains. Wet the bar and simply rub the stain, working it in well. Let it sit a few minutes. This spotter still works even if allowed to dry on the fabric. Great for ring-around-the-collar and perspiration stains.

Ink Away™: Ink and marker can be a challenge to remove, but this product, made by the makers of Goo Gone™, really proves its worth. Follow package directions carefully and be sure to read the list of things *not* to use it on *before* you start.

Spot Shot® Instant Carpet Stain Remover: This one wins the prize for the most unusual laundry spotter, but it's *still* one of the Queen's favorite products. Yes, that's right, it's not just for carpet. It's also a great laundry prewash spotter—and boy does it work. It is safe for all colorfast washables and works in all wash temperatures. Spray the stained area thoroughly, saturating the stain. If the stain is difficult or stubborn, work it between your thumbs. Allow Spot Shot® to sit at least 60 seconds, then launder as usual. *Do not* allow it to dry on the fabric and do not use it on silks, fabrics labeled "dry clean only" or noncolorfast fabrics. This product works on oily stains, ink, pet stains, cola, shoe polish, lipstick, blood and others. A must-have in the laundry room.

Wine Away Red Wine Stain Remover™: Don't let the name fool you, this product is much more than a red wine stain remover. It works great on Kool-Aid™, grape juice, red pop, cranberry juice, orange pop, coffee and tea, as well as red wine. I even took red food coloring out of a shirt with it.

Wine Away™ is made from fruit and vegetable extracts and is totally nontoxic—I love that!

Zout® Stain Remover: This is a super-concentrated stain remover that works great on ink, blood, grease, fruit juice, grass and hundreds of other stains. A little goes a long way with this. Simply saturate the stain, work it in, wait 5 to 10 minutes, and then launder as usual.

7

Stain Removers That Are Hiding in Your Cupboard

You may not know this, but some of the very best spot and stain removers are things you use every single day! Not only do these stain removers work great—they're right at your fingertips!

Alcohol: Rubbing alcohol is great for grass stains and so much more.

Ammonia: The perspiration stain fighter.

Automatic dishwasher detergent: Keep this on hand as a bleach substitute and whitener/brightener even if you *don't* have a dishwasher. Liquid, powder, and tablet form all work well. If you choose the tablet, make sure it has dissolved before you add clothes. Pour directly on stain, or soak.

Baking soda: Removes odors.

Club soda: My favorite *Oh my gosh, how did I do that?* spotter. Use it on any fabric or surface that can be treated with water. A slight dabbing on dry-clean-only fabrics is also permissible, just be sure to test first! Use club soda on any spill—ask the waiter for some if you're dining out—dab it on and blot it off. Club soda keeps spills from becoming stains and brings the offending spill to the surface so it can be easily removed. It's totally safe. I always make sure to have a bottle on hand.

Cream of tartar: I bet you have some of this in the kitchen cupboard, but how often do you use it? Well, here's your chance. Mix cream of tartar with lemon juice and you have a wonderful bleach for white clothes spotted with food or other stains. It's even effective on many rust stains.

Denture-cleaning tablets: The cure-all for white table linens with food stains and white cotton with stains. Dissolve one tablet per ½ cup water. Pour directly on stain or spot.

Dishwashing liquid: A wonderful spotter, used undiluted on tough stains.

Glycerin: You can remove tar, tree sap (think Christmas tree), juice stains, mustard, ketchup and barbecue sauce.

Go-Jo Waterless Hand Cleaner®: Totally awesome for removing grease and oil, including shoe polish.

Hydrogen peroxide: 3 percent hydrogen peroxide is super for removing blood stains, especially if they are fairly fresh. It also is a wonderful bleaching agent for stubborn stains on white clothes. Combine ½ cup of hydrogen peroxide and 1 teaspoon of ammonia for an unbeatable stain removal combination. Make sure to use 3 percent and *not* the kind you use to bleach your hair!

Lemon Juice: This is nature's bleach and disinfectant. I don't know where we'd be without it. If you have spots on white clothes, apply some lemon juice and lay them in the sun. Apply a little more lemon juice prior to laundering, or prespray and launder as usual. This is really effective on baby formula stains.

Meat tenderizer: A combo of meat tenderizer (unseasoned, please, or you'll have a whole new stain!) and cold water is just the answer to protein-based stains such as blood, milk, etc.

Salt: Sprinkling salt on spilled red wine will keep the wine from staining until you can launder it. Mixed with lemon juice, salt will remove mildew stains.

Shampoo: Any brand will do. Cheap is fine. I save the small bottles from hotel/motel stays and keep them in the laundry room. Great for treating ring-around-the-collar, mud and cosmetic stains.

Shave cream: That innocent-looking can of shave cream in your bathroom is one of the best spot and stain removers available. That's because it's really whipped soap! If you have a spill on your clothes (or even your carpet), moisten the spot, work in some shave cream, and then flush it with cool water. If the offending spot is on something you're wearing, work the shave cream in and then use a clean cloth (a washcloth works fine) to blot the shave cream and the spot away. A quick touch of the blow-dryer to prevent a ring and you're on your way. The best thing about shave cream is that even if it doesn't work it won't set the stain, so the spot can still be removed later. Keep a small sample can in your suitcase when you travel. It's saved me more than once!

WD-40 Lubricant®: Check out your garage or the "fix-it" cupboard. If you don't have any, pick up a can the next time you're at the hardware store or home center. Why? Because we've all had those nasty grease stains and oil stains on clothes: salad dressing misses the salad and gets the blouse, or grease splatters when you are cooking—or crayon/lipstick/ Chap Stick® gets on your clothes! WD-40 is your answer. Spray some on, wait 10 minutes, then work in undiluted liquid dishwashing soap and launder as usual. Works well on everything *except* silk!

White vinegar: A great spotter for suede—used undiluted. It's also a wonderful fabric softener. Just put ¼ cup white vinegar in the final rinse. (And no, you won't smell like a salad!)

It's worthwhile to keep these things on hand. As you can see, most are inexpensive *and* have other uses. They'll make you the laundry Queen—or King!—in your home.

8

Bleach 101: Whiter Whites, Brighter Brights

Are you one of those people who thinks that directions are what you read to find out what you did wrong? Then pay attention. I'm going to give you my dos and don'ts of bleach basics.

DO ....

- Read the directions on the container of bleach.

- Check the labels on the fabric you wish to bleach.

- Test the bleach if you are unsure. To do this with chlorine bleach, mix 1 tablespoon of chlorine bleach with ¼ cup of cold water. Find a hidden area on the piece of clothing and place a drop of the solution on it. Leave this for a minute or two and then blot to determine if there is any color change.

- To test all-fabric bleaches, mix 1 teaspoon of the bleach with 1 cup of hot water. Again, place a drop on an inconspicuous area. Wait at least 15 minutes, blot, and check for any change in the color.

- Of course if any color change takes place you won't want to use that type of bleach on that type of fabric.

- Always be sure to rinse bleach out of fabric thoroughly.

DON'TS

- Absolutely never allow undiluted chlorine bleach to come in contact with fabrics.

- Never use any kind of bleach directly on fabric without testing it first.

- Never use more bleach than called for. It can damage fabrics and is wasteful too.

- NEVER use chlorine bleach and ammonia in the same wash! It can generate deadly fumes.

Now let's talk about the bleaches one by one.

Chlorine Bleach

The strongest, fastest-acting bleach available, chlorine bleach is very effective on cottons, linens, and some synthetics when used properly. Used improperly it can weaken cloth fibers, causing them to disintegrate. It can even cause holes. Always follow container directions with care, and never use chlorine bleach on silk, wool, spandex, acetate, fibers treated to be flame-resistant or dry-clean-only fabrics.

Most of us have had a bad experience with chlorine bleach, so use care. Never pour it on hand washables, and never pour it onto clothes that are in the washing machine. Pour it in the bleach dispenser, if your washing machine is so equipped, or into the washer while it is filling with water *before* adding the clothes. For hand washables, dilute it prior to adding the clothes and be sure to adjust the amount accordingly for the amount of water being used.

Name brands and store brands work the same, so purchase the product of your choice, or the one with the best price.

All-Fabric Bleach or Oxygen Bleach

This is a much milder form of bleach that works well on delicate fabrics or those requiring gentle care. It is slower-acting than chlorine bleach and is less effective in restoring whiteness to fabrics. It may be effective, though, through regular use. This bleach can be used on all fabrics, even silks, as long as the manufacturer's care tag does not say "no bleach." Add this bleach at the same time you add your detergent and do not pour directly on the clothes. More is not better, so measure, don't just pour.

A New Generation of Bleach

Soapworks has come up with a new generation of bleach that is effective, user friendly, and safe for use by people with allergies and asthma. It is hypoallergenic, nontoxic, biodegradable, 100 percent natural, safe for septic tanks, contains no chemicals, no dyes and no fragrances.

This product is called Brilliant™, and it is just that!

Created with hydrogen peroxide—which is the safest, natural whitener and brightener for fabrics—this bleach can be used effectively on whites and colored fabrics both. Clothes can be soaked safely for 24 hours or more without harm to either fabric or color.

Brilliant™ is also a softener, so no additional softening agent is required. Add ¼ cup to the washer as it fills with water. As with any bleach product, test in an inconspicuous area when in doubt.

Making Your Own Bleaching Agents

Yes, you *can* create your own forms of bleach with things you already have at home.

Lemon juice: Nature's bleach and disinfectant, lemon juice can be used to whiten clothes.

Take 1 gallon of the hottest water possible for the fabric you're bleaching and add ½ cup of bottled lemon juice or the slices of one or two lemons. Soak the clothes for 30 minutes or even overnight. This works especially well on white socks and underwear, and is safe for polyester fabrics. Don't use on silks, though.

Automatic dishwasher detergent: This is another wonderful bleaching agent for white clothes. Fill a bucket with the hottest possible water for the fabric you are working with, and add 2 tablespoons of any brand of automatic dishwasher detergent. Soak white clothes for 30 minutes or even overnight. Dump into the washer and launder with your detergent as usual.

To use this bleaching technique in the washer, fill the

machine with water and add ¼ cup to ½ cup of automatic dishwasher detergent. Agitate for several minutes and then add clothes. Soak as directed above and then add detergent and launder as usual.

Hydrogen peroxide: This can be used to bleach delicate items such as wool or wool blends. Soak them overnight in a solution of one part 3 percent hydrogen peroxide to eight parts cold water. Launder according to care directions.

Bluing

Bluing is a whitening and brightening agent that has been around for a long, long time. Available in liquid form, bluing contains blue pigment, which actually counteracts the yellowing that occurs in some fabrics. Always dilute this with water as directed on the bottle, and never pour directly on clothes or spill on other fibers or surfaces. Look for it in the laundry aisle at the grocery store. This product will even remove the yellow from gray hair!

9

Fabric Softeners—
The Soft Sell

Fabric softeners are used to make fabrics soft and fluffy, and to minimize static cling. They can also reduce wrinkling and make ironing easier.

Liquid softeners: These should be added to the final rinse cycle by the automatic dispenser (if your washing machine has one), or by hand if not. Carefully follow the directions on the label, and make sure to measure: too much is not better, nor is too little.

If using an automatic dispenser, add the softener then follow with an equal amount of water to help disperse the liquid softener. This will also help to eliminate softener spots on clothes.

Dryer-added softeners: These paper-thin sheets soften clothes, and they also work with the heat of the dryer to reduce static electricity in the load—which means that your dress won't cling to your panty hose and your trousers won't cling to your socks! I find store brands work just as well as higher-priced varieties, so go ahead and make your choice by fragrance or price. Whatever suits you.

By the way, if static cling is a problem (and it happens to the best of us), try smoothing your skirt with a damp pair of hands. A little bit of hand cream on top of your panty hose works well, too.

A word of advice. Dryer softener sheets can cause buildup on towels, and that can make them feel slippery and reduce their absorbency. Use the softener only once every two to three washings to avoid this.

Retired Softener Sheets

Once you have used the pesky little sheet, remember my earlier advice: use it to clean off the lint filter in the dryer before you toss it. Here are some other uses for those retired sheets.

• If you have a casserole or pan with burned-on food, fill with hot water, toss in a softener sheet for several hours (overnight is fine), and the burned-on food will slide right out.

• Run a needle and thread through the sheet to prevent static from tangling the thread.

• Wipe the television screen, venetian blinds, or any other surface that attracts dust with a used sheet to reduce the static electricity that attracts dust.

• Place a sheet in a coat pocket to avoid the shock you get when getting in and out of the car in winter.

• Place a used sheet in luggage, drawers, closets, trash-cans, under car seats, and in your laundry bag or hamper to provide a fresh scent.

• Tuck a used sheet into shoes before placing them in your luggage. Shoes will smell fresh and you can use the dryer softener sheet to buff shoes and remove dust after wearing.

• Polish chrome to a brilliant shine after cleaning.

• Use it to wrap Christmas ornaments or other fragile things before boxing for storage. The dryer sheet will protect them and you can wipe Christmas ornaments prior to hanging on the tree to reduce static electricity and repel dust.

• Wipe car dashboards with a used sheet to shine and repel dust.

Retired dryer fabric softener sheets have plenty of uses left, so don't waste them. And don't use new softener sheets for any of these purposes. Pick up a *used* or, as I like to call them, *retired*, sheet instead! I put my used dryer sheets in an empty tissue box I keep in the laundry room. This way they are always handy.

Making Your Own Dryer Fabric Softener Sheets

Believe it or not, you can make your own dryer fabric softener sheets. Simply take an old washcloth, mist it with 1 part of your favorite liquid fabric softener and 2 parts water, then toss it in the dryer with the clothes. Re-mist for each new load of clothes and occasionally launder it when doing towels to remove any softener buildup and soften the towels at the same time.

I keep a mixture in a small spray bottle on the shelf in the laundry room along with a few old washcloths. I find that ⅓ cup liquid fabric softener and ⅔ cup of warm water makes a good quantity. Shake prior to spraying on the cloth, and *always* label the bottle of any mixture you make yourself to keep it from accidentally being misused.

If your detergent already contains softener (read the label) you may not need additional softener unless you are getting a lot of static cling in your clothes.

Fabric Softener Spots on Clothes

No matter how hard you try, at some point you will probably pull out a load of clothes and find either blue spots from liquid fabric softener or "grease"-type spots from dryer softener sheets on your clothes. Here's what to do:

Liquid softener spots: If spotting occurs, wet the item and rub with undiluted dishwashing liquid, then rewash. Wetting and rubbing with shampoo seems to work too. Do *not* rub with laundry detergent. It won't remove the spot—in fact, it may set it in.

If liquid softener has been allowed to freeze, dissolve the required amount of softener with warm water before adding to the wash.

Dryer fabric softener sheet spots: If spotting occurs, rub the area with a wet bar of soap, such as Dove®, and then relaunder.

To avoid spots, place the sheet on top of the clothes in the dryer rather than mixing it in, and start the dryer immediately. Do not use the sheet when you are using the air fluff cycle without heat.

Important: Do *not* use dryer sheets on children's sleepwear or other garments labeled as flame-resistant as they may reduce flame resistance. These sheets are *not* nontoxic, so keep out of reach of children and pets to avoid accidental ingestion.

⑩
The Hard Truth About Water Softeners

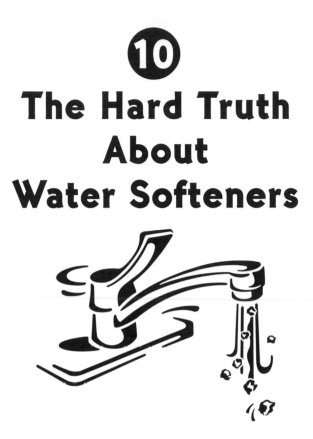

If you live in an area that has hard water you will be well acquainted with the graying or yellowing effect that hard water minerals can have on your clothes. You may also have noticed that, rather than suds in your washing machine, you have gray-looking water and, sometimes, scum on the water surface.

Not sure if you have hard water? You can check your local water supply office—they will tell you the degree of hardness in your water. If you have well water you might want to call a water treatment company. They'll be able to test your supply. Of course, you can also look out for these telltale signs:

- Fabrics look dull and gray.

- Fabrics feel stiff instead of soft.

- Soaps and detergents don't lather well.

- White residue appears around drains, faucets, and on glassware.

If your water is not too hard (less than 10.6 grains of hardness per gallon), you can help alleviate the problems associated with hard water by adjusting the amount of detergent you use. Again, start by using half the amount of detergent called for. You can also give your detergent a "kick" by using Arm and Hammer Washing Soda™, or Twenty Mule Team Borax™ along with your detergent, following package directions. These products are found in the laundry additive aisle at the grocery store or at discount stores. If you find that your clothes still do not have the degree of cleanness and softness that you desire, you may need to try a liquid softener that you can add to your laundry along with your detergent, or go to a mechanical means of softening.

Making Your Own Water Softener

Combine the following in a labeled one-gallon container. Plastic gallon milk jugs, washed well, work great.

½ lb. of Arm and Hammer Washing Soda™
¼ lb. of Twenty Mule Team Borax™
1 gallon of warm water

To use: Add 1 cup of the solution to each load of wash water along with your normal laundry detergent.

If you still find that your wash is dingy and you are not getting any lather from your bar soap in the shower, then you may need to turn to a mechanical softener which is attached to the house water system.

Starch and Sizing

Starches and sizing restore body to fabrics that have become limp through washing or dry cleaning. They also form a protective barrier to repel dirt. Fabrics such as cotton or linen respond particularly well to these products.

Starch: Comes in spray, liquid, and powder form. Liquid and powder starch should be combined with water—the directions on the package will tell you what proportions to use. Mix to a thick paste if you want your clothes to have a crisp starched appearance. A thinner consistency will give you a lighter look. You can also add starch to the final machine rinse if you like. Just be sure to follow the directions carefully.

The easiest form of starch is spray starch, which you apply while ironing. Just spritz it on the clothes and iron. It's that easy! Spray starches provide a light effect. Use powder or liquid if you prefer a heavier starch.

Sizing: A lighter cousin to starch, sizing is applied in the manufacturing process to provide protection and body to fabric. General wear, moisture, perspiration, and washing or dry cleaning will eventually break down the sizing, though; you may want to reapply it. Buy it in a spray can and spritz it on garments as you iron.

Do not use too much of these spray products. And don't use your iron on a high heat—the starch or sizing will flake off if you do.

⑫
Cry Me a River— The Color Ran!

Ever turned your underwear pink? Then you know what I'm talking about when I say that some dark colors bleed during initial washing. Not all colors are what we call "colorfast," so you must be careful to prevent the dye of one garment from running on to another.

Is It Colorfast?

How do you know if an item is colorfast? Test it! Try this simple colorfast test before you launder new fabrics. You'll save yourself a lot of time and heartache if you do.

• Place a drop of water on an inside seam or another inconspicuous spot. Blot with a white cotton ball or towel.

• If the cotton ball remains clean, it is safe to wash with other clothes. If it picks up some color from the fabric then you must wash the garment separately.

Be careful not to drip-dry fabrics that are not colorfast. The color can streak. Instead, roll these clothes in a towel to absorb excess moisture, then hang to dry, away from other fabrics.

Uh-Oh . . .

What happens if a pair of new black socks were somehow washed with your favorite white blouse? Fugitive color happens, that's what! Don't despair. Some products can help you do away with color runs.

Synthrapol®*:* This is a wonderful product used by quilters to eliminate color runs in quilts. Used in a basin or in the washing machine, it will remove fugitive color without damage to the original color or fabric. In simple terms, if you washed a white T-shirt with a red T-shirt and the white T-shirt turned pink, Synthrapol® will remove the pink and return the shirt to its original white.

Synthrapol® works best on cottons, but I've had success with polyester and blends too. Try it in an inconspicuous spot first, unless the item is a total loss and you feel you've got nothing to lose. This is a fairly strong chemical, so be sure to follow the directions carefully.

Carbona® Color Run Remover: One box of Carbona® will restore a whole wash load of clothes dyed from mixed-wash bleeding. You *must* test the fabric to be sure that it's colorfast, otherwise the garment's original color will be removed along with the fugitive color. Follow the directions carefully and use great care. This, too, is a strong chemical. It may be harmful to synthetic materials, denim, or bright, fluorescent and khaki colors. Zippers, buttons, etc., may become discolored, so you might want to remove what you can prior to treatment.

Retayne®: A color fixative for cottons, Retayne® is an interesting product that you should use *before* washing a garment that is likely to bleed. Just think of this as an ounce of prevention.

For best results, treat the garment with Retayne® prior to laundering for the first time. Not only will this prevent bleeding, it will also help to keep colors brighter, longer. Again, as with everything, try in an inconspicuous area first and read the directions carefully.

Important: All three of these products contain chemicals that can be harmful to children and pets, so please make sure to take adequate storage precautions.

⑬
You Can Be a Rescuer of Things That Reek!

Odor can be a big laundry problem. There are a number of perfumed products that claim to remove odor and leave fabric fresh-smelling. It's been my experience, however, that most of these products just mask smells. I don't know about you, but I'd rather not have lilac-scented perspiration.

Putting white vinegar in the final rinse will remove some odors. But for difficult odors, such as smoke, urine, pet, garlic, gasoline, etc., you need a much stronger product. I highly recommend ODORZOUT™, a 100 percent natural product with no odor of its own. Use it dry or wet. It doesn't cover-up odors—it actually absorbs them! And it's safe for people with asthma or allergies too!

To use dry, sprinkle directly on clothes that have an offensive odor, and allow them to sit for several hours. Intense odors, such as gasoline, can be treated for several days with no harm to the fabric. Just make sure you allow air to circulate—the product won't work in an enclosed space.

To use wet, simply fill the washing machine and add 1 to 2 teaspoons of ODORZOUT™. Agitate for a minute and then add the clothes and your detergent. Launder as usual.

ODORZOUT™ is great when sprinkled on pet bedding several hours before laundering. You can also use it to control odor in hampers and diaper pails. It is safe and nontoxic for use around kids and pets, which is a big plus.

Try the ODORZOUT™ Pouch as well. You can put them in empty shoes to eliminate smells, and in cupboards and drawers to keep odors at bay. I love the convenience.

Another good general odor remover for laundry is Twenty Mule Team Borax Laundry Additive™. Add this to any odorous load of laundry. Just follow the directions on the box. This product is safe for all washables.

Remember, if it stinks, it's best to treat it immediately, before the odor can be passed on to other items.

14

Care Labels: What Are They Good For?

When you examine a label, do you look at the size and nothing else? Well, you're missing out on a lot of valuable information. Care labels are very important. You should read each and every one of them before you purchase a garment, and each time you have it cleaned.

The Federal Trade Commission (FTC) requires manufacturers to attach a permanent label to textile garments indicating directions for care. This label must be easily located. It should not separate from the garment, and it should remain legible during the lifespan of the garment. The label must warn about any part of the recommended care method that would harm the garment or other garments being laundered or dry-cleaned with it. It must also specify if a garment cannot be cleaned without damage.

Symbols may also appear on a care label to supplement written instructions. When a garment carries an international symbol tag, all care methods will usually be listed.

May I Remove the Care Label? Garments are required by law to have a care label attached at the time of sale. Of course, no law can take into account a woman wearing a little black dress with a big white care label hanging out the back. Removing the care tag does entail some risk, though; you may forget the proper cleaning instructions and your dry cleaner will not have access to some valuable information.

If you do remove care labels, mark them with a description of the item and put them in a safe place where they can be easily located. You might remember today that your favorite summer dress should be washed in cold water and laid flat to dry, but by next summer you may have forgotten this entirely. A corkboard in the laundry room is wonderful. Care directions will be at your fingertips and at those of other family members who may surprise you by doing the laundry sometime. Remove labels from the board when you no longer have the item.

Cleaning Instructions

Dry clean: A garment marked "dry clean only" can be cleaned using normal dry-cleaning fluid found in any commercial or coin-operated dry-cleaning establishment. Be aware that dry cleaning, despite its name, is not necessarily dry. Water may be involved in the process, whether by moisture added to the fluid, or by steam press or steam air-form finishing.

Professionally dry clean: If your garment is marked "professionally dry clean," then it is restricted to the dry-cleaning methods possible only in commercial dry-cleaning plants. A label marked "professionally dry clean" must be accompanied by further information, such as "use reduced moisture," "low heat," or "no steam finishing." Your dry cleaner should be alert to these labels, but there's no harm in pointing them out.

Machine wash: Indicates use of either a commercial or home washing machine. Other information may be included, such as specific washing temperatures, size of load, or drying instructions.

Does "washable" mean it can also be dry-cleaned? If a garment care label says "washable" it may be safely dry-cleaned—and it may not! Unfortunately, there is no way of telling from the label. A manufacturer is required to list only one safe method of cleaning, no matter how many other methods can be safely employed. And be warned: Manufacturers are not required to alert you to care procedures that *may not* be safe.

15

Doing the Laundry Sorting Boogie

Now that we have our products ready to spot, bleach, launder, and soften, it's time to actually do the laundry! Make it easy on yourself. Sort *before* you start to wash.

Some people like the "grab and stuff" laundry method: grab the clothes—no matter what fabric or color—and stuff them into the machine, as many as you can at one time. These people are easy to recognize. They're the ones with pink underwear, color-streaked clothes, shrunken sweaters, short pants, and clothes that are otherwise "challenged."

Sort your laundry for best results. You'll thank me for this advice, I assure you.

Separate

- Dark fabrics from white and light-colored fabrics.
- Lightly soiled clothes from heavily soiled garments such as work clothes.
- Fabrics by water temperature (hot—warm—cold).
- Fabrics that will shed lint on other fabrics (terry cloth, corduroy, etc.).
- Lingerie, hose, and delicate fabrics that should be washed in a mesh bag.
- Clothes that may have fugitive color and bleed onto others.

Do This *Before* You Wash

- Button buttons.
- Hook bras.
- Zip zippers.
- Tie sashes, cords, straps etc., to prevent tangling.
- Check pockets for coins, tissues, pens, etc.
- Remove anything on the garment that cannot be washed.
- Repair tears so they don't become larger while agitating.

Now It's Time to Pretreat

- Check for spots, spills, stains, etc., before putting a load of clothes into the washer.
- Pretreat these with one of the spotters you'll find in Chapters 5 and 6, or go to the stain removal guide for help.

• Soak heavily soiled garments before laundering. *Do not* soak wool, spandex, silk, or fabrics that are not colorfast.

Mark the Spot

Use a brightly colored clothespin to mark the stain, or use a rubber band and wrap it around the area that needs to be spotted prior to laundering. Have family members do this *before* they put their clothes into the hamper. This will make spots and stains easier to locate and easier to treat. Spots will be obvious, so you don't need to examine each article as you sort.

Now You're Ready to Wash!

Add detergent to the washer as it fills up with water. If you are using cold water with powdered detergent and you have a problem with the detergent dissolving, mix it with a little hot water before adding it to the machine—or consider switching to a liquid detergent.

• Add additional laundry aids such as bleach, water softener, laundry booster, etc.

• Load the machine, but do not overload. If you stuff too many garments into the machine the clothes will not clean well, and they'll have more wrinkles too.

• Make sure your load is balanced—not all bunched on one side of the agitator—especially if you are washing one large or heavy item, such as a blanket or bath mat.

• Remember: don't leave the house while you're doing laundry.

If you have room in your laundry or closet areas, provide several different colored laundry baskets for family members to sort dirty clothes as they are removed—a basket for whites, colors, jeans (if your family wears a lot of them), and delicates. You'll be off to a good start and the whole laundry sorting boogie will go faster. Use these baskets after washing to hold clothes that need to be folded and to carry clothes that can be put away.

16

Know When to Hold 'Em, Know When to Fold 'Em

Normally I don't like to use the f-word . . . but not everything can be hung on a hanger. There are some things that simply must be *folded*. Don't worry, though. You don't have to be the empress of elbow grease to quickly fold clothes and put them away.

It's best to hang items that wrinkle easily, such as cotton, rayon, etc. Blouses, dress shirts and dresses that are not knit are best on a hanger. Knits are best folded.

Consider the space your clothes have to fit into before you fold them.

If, for example, drawer space is at a premium in your

house, consider rolling things such as underwear, T-shirts, socks, towels, etc. You can fit more into a drawer or cupboard that way, and wrinkles will be minimal. Rolled clothes also save lots of room in your suitcase—an added bonus for frequent travelers.

Sweaters and sweatshirts are best folded, and you will never have shoulder dimples, either. To fold, lay the garment facedown and fold each side to meet in the middle at the back. This will avoid a line running down the center of your garment. Fold the sleeves down the back of the garment, then fold the garment in half lengthways. These items can also be rolled effectively.

Socks can be rolled toe to top. You might also want to consider investing in draw dividers made specifically for socks and hose. You will never find your socks in a tangled mess, or worse still, missing. Colors will be obvious and easy to pick out.

And by the way, just to set the record straight, washers and dryers positively *do not* eat socks. Nor is there a sock monster in your utility room who steals one sock! Missing socks can sometimes be found wedged between the drum and the machine. Check your pant legs and shirt sleeves, and check the dryer hose, too. I once found a lonely sock on the driveway—it had tried to escape by shimmying out the dryer hose and up through the vent!

Fitted sheets *can* be tamed. Fold them in half lengthwise, then fold each curved end into the middle. Now you have a square end to work with. Fold in half again and then either roll or continue to fold to the size that best fits your storage area. If you don't mind the same sheets on the bed each week, wash them, dry them, and put them back on straightaway and you will *never* have to fold them again!

Fold rubber or latex-backed rugs with the fabric side in to prevent the backing from sticking together during storage. Consider using hooks on the back of the closet doors for robes and nightclothes. Don't use suction hooks, though. They're not strong enough to hold clothes.

If doing underwear for multiple family members together, consider buying different brands for each person to make sorting and folding go faster. Try this with socks too.

Keeping a spring-type curtain rod or shower rod set up in the laundry room makes it easy to hang clothes as you remove them from the dryer. Let each person come and claim their own hanging clothes and basket of ready-to-fold or folded clothes. This will cut your laundry time way down. A quick reminder: If the kids have to fold their own clothes, don't let them defeat your system and dress out of the laundry basket all week instead of folding and putting away their things. Otherwise, they will throw the dirty clothes on the floor all week!

Good laundry habits are easy to learn, especially when they become routine.

17

Taking the Dread Out of Dry Cleaning

Not everything we wear can be laundered, and that means a trip to the dry cleaner and the dreaded game of "will that spot come out?" Most people end up at the dry cleaner because they have clothing stains they can't get out themselves. Luckily for us, professional dry cleaners, with their special solvents, equipment and training, can remove some of the most disastrous-looking stains fairly simply. Successful stain removal depends on three things: the nature of the stain; the type of fabric; and the colorfastness of the dye. Remember to check your care labels. Not all fabrics and dyes are made to withstand the use of cleaning or stain removal agents.

Invisible stains: Many stains that are caused by food, oily substances, or beverages may become invisible when they dry. Later on, with exposure to heat or the passage of time, a yellowish or brownish stain will appear. You have probably seen this on clothes you have hung away and pulled out months later. This is caused by the oxidation of the sugar in the staining substance. It is the same thing that makes an apple turn brown once it is peeled and exposed to the air.

You can be a better dry-cleaning customer and help your dry cleaner do a better job for you by pointing out such stains when you take a garment in to be cleaned. The cleaner often treats these stains prior to cleaning, much as you prespot your laundry at home. This pretreatment is vital since the heat of drying or finishing may set the stain, making it impossible to remove.

When an oily substance is exposed to heat or ages in a piece of clothing for a long period of time, it oxidizes. This type of stain can be recognized by its irregular shape on the fabric. Oily stains can be removed easily during the dry-cleaning process provided they have not been there for an extended period of time. Once they are yellow or brown, they are almost impossible to remove.

Perspiration stains: Perspiration can also cause problem stains, especially on silk and wool clothes. Perspiration left in a silk garment can eventually cause deterioration of the fibers.

Repeated exposure to perspiration and body oils can leave clothing with a permanent yellow discoloration and even an offensive odor. Perspiration can react with the dye in the fabric, making it even more difficult to remove the stain.

If you perspire heavily, have your clothes cleaned more frequently, especially in the warmer months.

Important Reminders

Make sure that you point out any unusual care instructions to your cleaner, and make sure that you point out spots and spills, identifying them wherever possible.

• Whether you are doing the cleaning yourself or a professional is doing it, treatment of spots and spills with the right spotter is essential.

• If you remove the care tag, it's a good idea to label it clearly—that is, identify the garment to which it belongs— and pin it to a corkboard in your laundry room for future reference.

Now the part we never want to hear—the dry cleaner's responsibility. Dry cleaners are responsible for attempting to remove stains in accordance with professional practice. Sadly, not all stains can be removed, despite the dry cleaner's best efforts.

The more information you give to your dry cleaner and the sooner a garment is brought in, the greater the chance of success in stain removal.

The Dirt on Home Dry-Cleaning Kits

You've seen them—those home dry-cleaning kits available in all the stores. What are they good for? Well, if you expect to open the dry-cleaning bag and find clean, sharply pressed clothes straight from the dryer, you'll be disappointed. If, however, you want to extend the time between professional dry cleanings, these kits may be for you.

I have found home dry-cleaning kits to be effective on items such as sweaters, cut velvet, velvet, dry-clean-only blouses—and those garments that are delicate and hard to hand wash and lay flat to dry. They are also great for freshening small blankets, bedspreads, comforters and draperies.

Do not force a large bedspread or blanket into the bag. It will be filled with wrinkles when you remove it.

Home dry-cleaning kits do work on suits, although you'll give up the sharply pressed finish. (You may even find occasional spotting on the suit's lining.)

All of these kits come with treated cloths and reusable dryer-safe bags. Some come with separate spotting solution and spotting blotters. They all work relatively the same way:

First, you spot the garment, either with the same sheet that you toss in the bag during the cleaning process, or with a separate spotting liquid. Spotting the garment well is important because, as we all know by now, heat can set stains. Take your time with the spotting procedure and look over the garment well.

I tested a group of kits to see how well they worked on spots (I think spot removal is probably what we're all most concerned with) and found that Custom Cleaner™ stood out. I put lipstick on the lapels of the King's blazer (*my* lipstick, you understand), and found that some of the dry-cleaning kits did not remove it. Custom Cleaner™ did, though—and then removed the stain the other kit left behind! I'm not big on fragrances either, but I found Custom Cleaner™ to have a clean, fresh smell. Not only that . . . the kit is convenient to use. Another plus!

Carefully follow the directions on the kit you have selected. Do not overcrowd the dryer bag or your clothes will be very wrinkled and require a lot of work with the iron—and that defeats the purpose.

Special Hints from the Palace

• Remove the clothes from the dryer bag immediately, and hang or fold them—whichever is appropriate. Some pressing may be required, depending on the type of fabric.

• Do not use any bag other than that which is provided in the kit, and do not use any additional cleaning chemicals.

• If you don't like the odor of perfume fresheners, check out each kit individually and try several. Some have more perfume than others.

• Again, follow the directions closely.

Are these kits worth the money? Ultimately, that's up to you to decide. If you have a lot of things you want to freshen between cleanings, and if that crisp, pressed look is not vital to you, then yes, give them a try. If, however, your wardrobe consists mostly of business suits and crisply creased trousers, you will probably be disappointed. Will these kits replace your regular trips to the dry cleaner? I don't think so. And I don't think they were intended to.

19
Final Thoughts on Dry Cleaning

I am frequently asked about dry cleaning items such as drapes, bedspreads, comforters, covers on upholstered cushions, slipcovers and antique items. Here are some final thoughts.

Draperies: Dry cleaning or professional laundering can prolong the life of your draperies and valances. With proper care, draperies can be expected to last from three to five years. Unfortunately, environmental conditions such as humidity, exposure to sunlight, and water damage from rain and condensation can discolor and weaken fabric, leaving draperies vulnerable to shredding when they are agitated during the cleaning process. Age, moisture, light, heat and nicotine can also damage draperies and turn them yellow.

Shrinkage is a big concern for draperies that have not been preshrunk, especially cottons and rayons. Your dry cleaner has stretchers to help eliminate this problem.

Distortion and fabric stiffening can also occur during the cleaning process. This depends on the fiber, weave, and design of your drapes. In addition, some draperies have a reflective coating that may not make it through the dry-cleaning process.

Talk with your dry cleaner *before* you have your draperies cleaned. Examine your draperies together. Be clear in your expectations and be honest as to the age of your drapes. Otherwise . . . it's curtains!

Bedspreads and comforters: Many bedspreads and comforters should be dry-cleaned or professionally laundered. Check for care instructions at the time of purchase so you know what is recommended. Tailored and quilted pieces are best done professionally.

Be sure to include all matching pieces when you have the bedspread or comforter cleaned. That way colors will remain uniform.

Upholstery and slipcovers: Upholstery is usually cleaned in place by professional cleaners, such as those who do carpet cleaning. These professionals will be able to maintain the color of your upholstery so that it matches the rest of your furniture.

So, why do cushion covers have zippers if we can't take

them off and dry clean or launder them? It is to allow for foam replacement, *not home cleaning.* Once you remove these covers, it is almost impossible to put them back on evenly with the seams straight. My best advice? Never remove and launder cushion covers.

If slipcovers are removed for dry cleaning or laundering, you need to be aware of whether they were preshrunk and what the shrinkage factor is. Check at the time of purchase.

It's a good idea to have slipcovers cleaned by professionals. They can ensure that the proper size machine is used and that there is no crowding, which can set in wrinkles. They also have the right equipment for touch-up pressing.

Antique fabrics: These are your treasures. They belonged to mom or grandmother or a favorite aunt. You love them, you treasure them, and now they are dirty.

Antique quilts, linens and fabrics require great care during the cleaning process. Not every cleaner is equipped for this so you may have to check around. Let your cleaner know right away that the item is very old and treasured. Proper cleaning by a careful professional might just well restore an aged and discolored piece.

Word of mouth is the best great way to find a good quality dry cleaner. Don't be afraid to ask around. Ask, too, what the cleaner's policy is on damaged items.

Prolong the Life of Your Fabrics

• Bear in mind that closely woven fabric is more durable than loosely woven fabric.

• Consider sun exposure when selecting fabrics. If you are putting drapes at a sunny window, look at acrylic, polyester and glass fibers.

• Read all the care instructions immediately. If you don't want to be bothered with a lot of care, select another item.

• Rotate drapes at windows that are the same size to vary exposure to light.

• Be sure your cleaner knows what your care label recommends.

• Regular cleaning can prolong the life of all fabrics. Clean your household items on a regular schedule.

20

Ironing and Ironing Boards: Taking the Heat

Nobody likes to iron, but occasionally, no matter how carefully you launder and dry your clothes, you're going to have to iron them too. Ironing can be a nasty chore, but I have some ways to make it easier. Just think of me as Chairman of the Ironing Board!

First of all, if you have to iron, do it in a place you enjoy. Set up the ironing board in the family room or somewhere you can watch television as you work, or near the stereo where you can listen to some music or a book on tape. You might even like to set it up in a room where the family is gathered so that you can all visit as you work. You can also enlist family members to hang up and put away their clothes as you iron them. (And don't assume I'm talking to mom. Dad should be able to do the ironing just as well!)

Now to the basics.

Cleaning Your Iron

Irons without nonstick finishes: If the iron has a silver sole plate (the metal will be shiny), that usually means it does not have a "nonstick" finish. To clean these irons, heat the iron to hot on the nonsteam setting, and run it over table salt sprinkled on a brown paper grocery bag. You can remove residue by using white, nongel toothpaste on a damp, soft cloth. Rinse well.

For really heavy buildup, or where fabric has burned to the bottom of a cold iron: protect the body of the iron by covering it with aluminum foil, then spray the sole plate with oven cleaner. Wait 10 minutes, rinse, and clean out the holes on the bottom of the iron with pipe cleaners or cotton swabs.

Rinse the bottom well and then, using steam, iron over an old towel or rag before using the iron on clothes.

Irons with nonstick finishes: Clean the sole plate with your favorite laundry prewash on a damp, soft cloth. Do this on a cool iron. Again, iron with steam over an old cloth before ironing clothes.

Cleaning the steam part of the iron: Fill the steam iron with equal portions of white vinegar and water. Let it steam for several minutes, then disconnect the iron and let it sit for one hour. Empty and rinse with clear water and iron over an old cloth, using steam.

Make the Most of Your Time at the Board

For energy-efficient ironing: Put aluminum foil between the ironing board and the cover—shiny side up. The foil will reflect the heat upward onto the garments you are ironing, so less effort is required by you!

To keep ironing boards clean longer: Spray the cover with spray starch and iron over it.

Ironing delicate fabrics: The secret to ironing these fabrics is to lay a "press cloth" over them and iron on that. Any old piece of lightweight cotton will work fine. Never lay a bare iron on delicate fabrics.

Collars: Iron both sides of the collar for a crisp, smooth finish. Start at the point and iron inward to the center to avoid pushing creases to the tip.

Seams and hems: To avoid creating a line over seams and hems, iron the garment inside out and stop just short of the seam or hemline.

Embroidery: Lay the piece of embroidery face down on a towel, and iron on the reverse side. That way you won't flatten the embroidery.

Large items: Before you start ironing, turn the ironing board around so that you are using the wide end rather than the point. You can cover more area as you iron this way. Fold items such as large tablecloths in half and iron one side, then fold in half again and iron the other two sides.

Dampening clothes: Our moms use to sprinkle clothes with water to help release the wrinkles and make ironing easier. This is still a good idea—especially with all the natural fibers we are wearing. Items that are too dry are very difficult to iron, so use a spray bottle to mist clothes that have dried. If clothes are heavily wrinkled, lay a damp towel on the ironing board and iron—with steam—over it. This works remarkably well on heavy trousers, jeans, etc.

The shoulder pad challenge: Try not to iron over shoulder pads or they will leave an ugly ring on the fabric. Just an additional note: Before you launder shoulder pads, tack the filling and the cover of the shoulder pad together so that it will not shift during the laundry and ironing process.

Steaming Strategies

• Test the iron first. If it sticks, jerks, or leaves a film on the ironing board cover, then stop—the iron needs to be cleaned before you iron clothes.

• Don't iron over zippers, buttons, or any lumps.

• Don't iron rubber, suede, leather, or stretch-type fabric.

• Don't iron dirty clothes or clothes that you have perspired in. It will set stains and damage the fibers.

• Use only a cool iron on synthetic fibers.

• When in doubt, start with a cool/warm iron.

• Test iron in an inconspicuous area. If in doubt, use a press cloth to avoid "shine" on the fabric surface.

• Always empty the water from the steam iron when you are done using it to prevent mineral buildup in the water reservoir.

Right Side, Wrong Side, Which Side?

• Iron cotton, net, or silky rayon right side up. These fabrics tend to wrinkle more than others, and ironing them on the *wrong* side will not get all the wrinkles out.

• Iron polyester on either side.

• Iron other garments on the wrong side of the fabric for best results. You'll avoid scorching, shine spots and other fabric damage.

Yikes! The Iron Was Too Hot! It's Scorched!

Try soaking the fabric in cold water overnight. That may remove the scorch mark.

On white fabrics, try saturating a cloth with 3 percent hydrogen peroxide, lay it over the scorch, and iron over it until the mark is removed. *Do not* use this method on colored fabric.

Refer to the Spot and Stain Removal Guide for more ways to treat scorch marks.

Part II
....
PALACE
PREDICAMENTS

㉑ Work Clothes

Dirty, greasy work clothes should never be washed with other clothes. Soil may transfer to the other clothes.

Prespotting stains is essential. Treat spots with a good spotter or Spot Shot Instant Carpet Stain Remover®. It's very effective on grease and oil. Launder in the hottest water you can for the fabric type, using a long wash cycle and adding ½ cup of washing soda along with your detergent.

If grease and oil are a major problem, spray the areas with WD-40 Lubricant® and wait 10 minutes. Work in undiluted dishwashing liquid and launder as usual.

Go-Jo Waterless Hand Cleaner® is also an effective degreasing agent. Work it into the spot and then launder as usual.

If dust and mud are a concern, prewash the clothes with the hottest possible water and ½ cup of washing soda and ½ cup of Twenty Mule Team Borax™. After the cycle is complete, add laundry detergent and launder as usual.

For heavily soiled, greasy work clothes, try pouring a can of Coke® in the washer with your detergent and launder as usual. The combination of cola syrup and sugar works like magic!

Good water and detergent circulation is important, so don't overcrowd the clothes in the washer.

Perspiration Stains: They're the Pits!

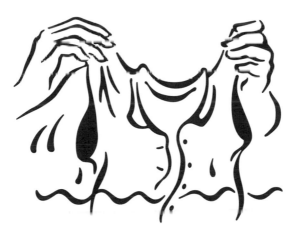

Perspiration will weaken fabrics, so treat vulnerable areas with care.

The best time to treat those invisible perspiration problems is right after you wear a garment for the first time, *before* you toss it in the washer.

Moisten the underarm area—or any other spot where perspiration stains are a problem—and work in a lather of Fels-Naptha Soap®. Once you've worked up a good lather, toss the garment in the machine and launder as usual.

Working Biz Activated Non Chlorine Bleach™ into the stained fabric is also effective. Just make sure to wet the offending area first!

Always treat perspiration areas on a garment *prior* to laundering. If odor is present, apply warm water to the area and work in Twenty Mule Team Borax™. Let sit 30 minutes or so, then launder.

ODORZOUT™ is also an extremely effective odor eliminator. Use it dry on those smelly areas. You can leave it on overnight—you can even put some in your clothes hamper.

If you already have stains, try dampening the fabric with warm water and working in laundry detergent and Biz™. Let that soak about 30 minutes and launder as usual.

I have found that soaking garments (whites or colors) in Brilliant Bleach™ from Soapworks is very effective for removing underarm stains.

You can also try to clean existing stains with heated white vinegar. Spray it on the fabric and then work in Twenty Mule Team Borax™. This works well on odor as well as stains.

If the fabric has changed color, try spraying with sudsy ammonia, let sit about 15 minutes, then launder as usual.

Bear in mind that yellowed or discolored fabric may be damaged. The garment may not be salvageable.

Treat everything prior to washing for the first time and do try switching brands of antiperspirant. Never wear shirts or blouses more than one day if you have a perspiration problem. You may find that wearing natural fibers such as cottons will be less of a problem than polyester and polyester blends. If your problem is serious you may want to try underarm shields. They trap moisture before it can reach the fabric. They can be removed and thrown away each day, and can't be seen through the garment. Look for them in lingerie stores and in catalogs.

㉓ Socks and Panty Hose

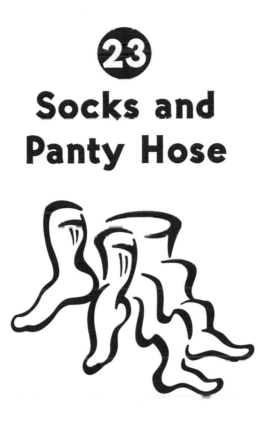

*F*olklore: If the legs of stockings, panty hose, leggings or socks intertwine on a clothesline or in a dryer, the owner of the garment is assured of joy and happiness.

Socks

White socks: To get white socks really clean, soak them for an hour in one gallon of hot water and 2 tablespoons of automatic dishwasher detergent. Pour the socks and soaking solution into the washer and launder as usual and they'll be clean and bright like you've never imagined.

You can also whiten socks by soaking in hot water to which you have added the slices of 1 lemon or ½ cup of lemon juice. Soak several hours or overnight. Put the socks in the washer and launder as usual.

Foot odor: Turn your socks into sweet-smelling odor beaters by adding ¼ cup of baking soda to one gallon of water. Spin the socks in the washer without rinsing out the baking soda solution. Dry as usual.

To increase the life of your panty hose: Dip them in water, wring them out, put them in a plastic bag, and freeze them solid. When you remove them from the freezer, let them thaw and dry completely. They'll be ready to wear and they'll last longer! Do this before you wear them for the first time.

To increase the elasticity in panty hose: Add 2 tablespoons of white vinegar to the rinse water.

To wash panty hose with ease in the washer: Use an old panty hose leg to hold a pair of good panty hose. Just knot the end of the panty hose leg at the top so the panty hose won't come out during washing. Adding some fabric softener to the rinse will lubricate the fibers and make the hose last longer and cut down on electricity. Out of softener? Use some hair conditioner!

Buy two, get one free: If you are down to your last pairs of panty hose and they all have runs in one leg, take two pairs of panty hose, cut off the damaged legs, and combine the two remaining "half pairs" to make one good pair! And if they happen to be control top, you've got double the tummy control!

24
Getting in the Swim

Swimwear is expensive, but correct care, washing and storage will ensure a long life.

Always read the care label before buying swimwear. This way you will be prepared for whatever care is required.

After swimming in a chlorinated pool, soak your suit for 15 minutes or so in cold water with a little liquid fabric softener. Rinse in cold water, then wash in cool water with mild detergent. Rinse well again and dry in the shade. Chlorine is very hard on fabrics, weakening them and changing the color, so be sure to rinse the suit as soon as you can. Never put your suit away without rinsing it out first.

If the suit has been worn in saltwater, soak it for a few minutes in cold water to remove the salt, then wash in cold water with mild detergent. Rinse well and dry in the shade.

Fold the suit in shape once it's dry. Store in tissue or in a perforated plastic bag for winter. (A perforated bag will allow the fabric to breathe.)

Hats and
Handbags

Y ou can't toss these in the washing machine. But you can
still clean them.

Leather bags: Clean these quite easily with a cloth that
you have wrung out in warm water and lathered with a bar
of moisturizing face soap, such as Dove®. Rub well, rinsing
the cloth as needed and working the soap in until all dirt has
been removed. Buff well with a soft cloth.

You may also polish the bag with leather cream or polish, following the directions on the container. Laying the
bag in the sun for 15 minutes or so will allow the polish to
absorb better.

Use your vacuum attachments to remove lint from the lining of your handbag, and spot with Energine Cleaning Fluid® where necessary. Again, use the blow-dryer to prevent rings.

Never store leather bags in plastic. Wrap in cloth or tissue. Never store leather and plastic or vinyl bags together. The leather will bleed color on to the other bags, ruining them.

Patent leather bags: Use a little petroleum jelly on a soft cloth to buff these to a brilliant shine. Buff once more with a clean, dry cloth.

Plastic or vinyl bags: These bags should be washed with a soft cloth or sponge and a mild soap or all-purpose cleaner. Rinse well and buff. If you want to restore the shine, apply a little spray furniture polish to a soft cloth and buff.

Suede bags: Brush suede bags frequently using a suede brush. Grease marks can be removed with a little dry-cleaning fluid, such as Energine®, or try a little undiluted white vinegar on a soft cloth. Brush the nap into position and allow to dry out of the sun, then brush again.

If the nap is severely flattened, steam the bag lightly over a pan of boiling water. Do not allow the bag to become too wet. Air-dry and then brush well.

Evening bags: Clean these gently with a soft cloth and some dry-cleaning fluid. Dry well by blotting or using the blow-dryer. Beaded bags can be lightly dusted with talcum powder to absorb dirt. Enclose the bag in a towel, wait 24 hours and then gently brush. Use care to not loosen threads holding the beads.

Heads Up

Caps: Clean soiled baseball caps the easy way by putting them in the dishwasher on the top rack. Run through the entire cycle, take out and allow to air dry. Washed this way, they will retain their shape. Works well for crowns too!

Hats that are not washable can be cleaned by using a soot-and-dirt removal sponge, available at hardware stores and home centers. Rub the dry sponge over the soiled areas of the hat, as if you were erasing with a large eraser. Do this outside or over a trash container or sink. Continue to work until you have removed all the soiling you possibly can. This is effective for felt and cowboy-style hats, too.

Cool water and shampoo work well on nylon or knit caps. Add a few drops of hair conditioner to rinse water to soften and condition the fibers. My Canadian friends will be pleased to know that this method works well on toques!

26
Ties: Don't Let Them Tie You in Knots

Ties are generally not washable, which is a shame because nothing gets more food spills and dipped into more things than ties. This does not mean that you can't successfully spot clean them, though.

If you have a tie with a food or beverage spill, first slip a pad of paper toweling in the opening between the front and the back of the tie. This will prevent the spot from forcing its way through the tie. Using Energine Cleaning Fluid®, moisten a soft, light colored cloth (think washcloth) and blot the spotted area. As the toweling absorbs the spot and the Energine®, change it to a clean, dry section of the pad.

Continue to blot until the spot is removed; then—and this is important—use your blow-dryer to dry the spot quickly to avoid a moisture ring.

When ironing a tie, lay it flat on the ironing board and cover with a press cloth (a lightweight towel will work) and press it with steam. Hang to dry completely. When storing ties, hang them or roll them (great for travel) to prevent wrinkles and creases.

27

Snap, Zip, and Hook! (No, It's Not a New Breakfast Cereal!)

The best advice I can give you is zip your zippers, snap your snaps, hook your hooks, and button your buttons.

If you don't, you run the risk of catching, pulling, or tearing fabric, damaging the interlocking mechanism (zipper) and pulling the buttons off during the washing process.

Just Zip It!

If you have a zipper that sticks and doesn't want to pull up, rub it with a little soap, paraffin, or candle wax. This will lubricate the teeth and get it moving.

If your zipper on slacks, skirts, etc., doesn't want to stay up, add a button, snap, or some Velcro just above it.

To give your zipper a little extra "stick," spritz it with hair spray. That will help it stay zipped.

Button Bonus

To keep buttons from falling off, dab a little clear nail polish on the thread in the center of the button. This will keep the thread from wearing through so easily.

For buttons that get hard wear, stitch them on with dental floss. It may not be as pleasing to the eye as thread, but the buttons won't fall off!

28

Beads and Sequins: Let's Face the Music and Dance

Laundering: Some sequined and beaded clothes can be washed. Here's how to keep them looking great:

- Button them completely prior to laundering.

- Turn clothes inside out prior to laundering.

- If machine washable, use only the gentle cycle set for approximately 2 or 3 minutes, with cold water and mild detergent.

• If the item is hand washable, use mild laundry soap or a little shampoo and cold water.

• Put a little hair conditioner in the final rinse if the garment is knitted.

• Always hang to dry or lay flat—never dry in the dryer.

Freshening: Spritz lightly with undiluted vodka under the arms and around the neck and cuffs. Hang to dry.

Spills: Many beaded outfits are labeled "spot clean only." Use a little club soda or Energine Cleaning Fluid®. Apply any moisture sparingly and then use a blow-dryer to dry the spot quickly to avoid a moisture ring.

㉙
Furs:
Real and Synthetic

If you have a fur coat, you know who you are, so no lectures.

Any fur garment that is worn regularly should be cleaned regularly too. This means once a year by a professional cleaner who specializes in fur. Best to have your fur cleaned just prior to storing it for the summer—this also applies to synthetic furs. A professional cleaner will remove stains, such as makeup, food, and beverages that can ruin fur. Keeping it clean will also deter moths.

It's a good idea to wear a soft scarf around the neck to keep stains and body oil away from a fur collar.

Treat small stains with a little Energine Cleaning Fluid®, on the fur and in the lining. Follow the directions on the can, and make sure to dry the areas that you spot clean with a blow-dryer in order to keep rings from forming. Always test in an inconspicuous spot first.

Hang furs and synthetic furs on well-padded hangers in a cloth bag. Don't use plastic. Shake the fur well when you take it from storage. You'll want to air it prior to wearing as well.

㉚
Sheepskin

If you have sheepskin rugs and car seats you probably know by now they are not machine washable. They can, however, be cleaned by a professional. Unfortunately, this can be costly.

If the sheepskin is not heavily soiled you can try to clean it with this method. Use a carpet cleaning powder, such as Host™ or Capture™. Both of these are excellent. They come with a machine to use on carpets, but you only need the chemical powder for sheepskin.

Sprinkle the cleaner onto the fleece and work it in well with your fingers, wearing rubber gloves. Roll up the sheepskin, slip it into a plastic bag and leave it for at least 8 hours, then shake or vacuum to remove the powder. Brush or comb the fleece and shake again before using.

If your sheepskin has a treated back and can be washed, follow the manufacturer's directions with care. Always use cool water and hang it to dry out of the sun. If you choose to dry it in the dryer, make sure to use the lowest possible heat setting. Always read the care label carefully prior to purchasing sheepskin.

Table Linens

Nothing makes a table look better than a beautiful table-cloth and napkins—but cleaning up after the meal can be a bit of a chore. Here are some foolproof ways to make the cleanup fast and easy.

Stain-proofing tablecloths: Spraying tablecloths with Scotchgard® Fabric Protector or a similar product prior to using will allow spills to wash out. Don't spray the cloth on top of a wood table. You'll spoil the finish.

Removing Stains from Tablecloths

Bleach white cotton and linen items. Soak colored items in heavy-duty detergent solution.

For white linens, you can also dissolve 2 denture-cleaning tablets in warm water. Spread out the stained area in a tub or sink. Pour on the solution and let soak for 30 minutes, then launder as usual.

Soaking stained table linens in Brilliant Bleach™ produces beautiful results. Soak until the stain is removed—even several days—without harming the fabric.

Removing red wine stains: These methods will work on any type of red stain, including red pop, cranberry juice, and fruit punches:

Always keep some white wine handy for red wine spills. Pour the white wine on the red wine and it will remove the stain. Do this as soon as you can.

Keep club soda on hand for red stains too. Pour the soda through the stain, preferably over the sink. Pretreat and launder as usual.

One of my very favorite products is called Wine Away Red Wine Stain Remover™, but don't let the name scare you, it works great on red pop, Kool-Aid™, cranberry juice, grape juice, red food coloring, and even tea and black coffee. It is made of fruit and vegetable extracts, so is totally nontoxic and easy to use.

Removing dried tea and black coffee stains: For tea stains, drape the stained item over a bowl or sink. Sprinkle with Twenty Mule Team Borax™ until the entire stain is covered. Pour a kettle full of hot water around the stain, working toward the center. Repeat if necessary and then launder as usual. For dried coffee stains, treat with a solution of 50 percent glycerin and 50 percent warm water. Rinse and blot well. Treat with laundry presoak prior to laundering.

Stains on cloth napkins: The most common stain on cloth napkins is lipstick. To remove this, spray the area with WD-40 Lubricant®, wait 10 minutes, then work in undiluted dishwashing liquid and launder as usual.

As an alternative, you can work in Go-Jo Waterless Hand Cleaner®, then launder as usual.

For food and beverage stains, treat with a commercial prespotter or one of the ones we made in Chapter 5, or use Spot Shot Instant Carpet Stain Remover®. Be sure not to let the spotters dry on the napkins before laundering.

You can also soak both white and colored napkins in Brilliant Bleach™ (Soapworks) without damaging the fabrics or colors.

Storing Tablecloths Wrinkle-Free

Instead of folding tablecloths, fold minimally lengthwise and then roll the cloth. It takes less room to store and will not wrinkle as easily, either. Hang cloths that wrinkle easily over a hanger covered with a fabric cover. A towel works well.

SPECIAL TIP ....

Never starch tablecloths before storing or they will yellow. If hanging, cover with a sheet or cloth. Don't use plastic as this too will cause yellowing.

Caring for Plastic and Vinyl Tablecloths

Clean plastic and vinyl tablecloths by wiping with a clean damp cloth and rinsing well. For stubborn stains, make a paste of lemon juice and cream of tartar and work it into the stain. Allow the paste to sit on the stain for a few minutes, then rinse. Let dry before folding.

Sprinkling clean plastic tablecloths with a little talcum powder before storing them will prevent stickiness and mildew.

32

Let the Light Shine: Cleaning Lampshades

*F**abric covered and stitched:*** I find the easiest way to wash these shades is in the bathtub! Put enough cool water in the tub to allow you to roll the shade on its side. Add some mild soap or detergent. Swirl the shade in the water/soap combination gently. Remove the soapy water and rinse the shade, using the same method—make sure the water is cool. Shake the shade gently to remove excess water and allow to dry in an upright position. Drying can be speeded up by using the blow-dryer. This works particularly well on thick and corded areas that dry more slowly.

Paper shades and shades with glue: You can't wet these shades, so your best bet is to vacuum them frequently with the duster brush on your vacuum. You can also purchase a soot-and-dirt removal sponge at the hardware store or home center. It's basically a big block eraser that you use dry to erase the dirt away. It works beautifully, just as long as you don't allow the shade to become heavily soiled. This eraser can also be used on washable shades.

Make sure the soot-and-dirt removal sponge is used dry on a dry object. You may wash the sponge, but be sure to let it dry before using it again.

Act Natural™ microfiber cloths also work well on lampshades. Dampen the cloth (only slightly damp, please) and wipe down the shade. It will remove dirt and hair without harming the shade.

Parchment shades: Dust or vacuum these shades regularly. You can use the soot-and-dirt removal sponge on these too. Even a slice of white bread with the crust removed will work! Rub the bread over the shade, preferably on the out side, and watch the dirt fall away with the crumbs.

Plastic shades: Wash these in warm water and mild soap. Dry them well and then restore the shine with spray furniture polish.

Scorch marks: Unfortunately, scorch marks on lampshades are not removable. The material is weakened by the heat and the damage is permanent. Take care when choosing bulbs. Scorch marks are generally caused by bulbs that are too large for the shade.

33
Slipcovers

Some slipcovers can be laundered in the washing machine. Just make sure to wash unusually large or bulky covers in a large, commercial washing machine.

Don't forget to test for colorfastness (see Chapter 12). Shake out or vacuum the slipcovers before washing and remember to follow the instructions on the care label.

Pretreat any spots or spills before laundering. Fels-Naptha Soap® worked into the arms and headrest will remove a lot of the greasy soiling. Wash in cool water and mild detergent and make sure to rinse well—twice if necessary. Do not over-crowd the slipcovers in the machine or you will be disappointed with the results.

Dry according to the care label. Heavy items such as these need room to breathe, so if you're going to hang your slipcovers to dry, make sure to spread them over several lines, spaced at least 12 inches apart. If you're using the dryer you should check and rearrange the covers frequently.

Press slipcovers with an iron heated to the appropriate temperature for the fabric type, and fit the covers back on the furniture while they are still slightly damp. Not only will they stretch more readily when damp, but they will shrink slightly as they dry, and that will draw out wrinkles and creases. When the covers are good and dry you may want to apply a light coating of fabric protector to help keep them soil-resistant.

34
Don't Throw in the Towel!

It's lovely to step out of the shower and wrap yourself in a clean, fluffy towel—what I call a *warm fuzzy*. Towels are pretty low maintenance; nevertheless there are some things you can do to keep them at their best. Read on . . . what follows is absorbing!

Washing towels in hot water with your favorite laundry detergent or soap will remove normal soiling. Add ½ cup of washing soda to a full load of towels if you want to kick your detergent up a notch and clean more effectively.

Presoaking heavily soiled towels is always a good idea. Soak them in hot water and ½ cup of Twenty Mule Team Borax™, and you will deodorize them as well!

Fabric softener will provide you with soft, fluffy towels, but overuse will make the towels less absorbent. Use softener every second or third time instead of every time you launder them. You can also use ½ cup of white vinegar as a softening agent. And no, the towels will not smell like vinegar!

Dark-dyed towels will lose a considerable amount of dye during their first several washings. If you have faded towels the same color as the new ones, wash them together to restore some of the color to the old batch. Adding 1 cup of table salt to the wash water the first time you launder dark towels will keep them from fading as quickly.

Do not wash dark towels and light towels together, ever! The light towels will pick up the color and fuzz from the dark ones, and the dark towels will end up with light-colored lint all over them.

Always wash new towels prior to using to remove the sizing and make them more absorbent. If you find yourself with towels that are slick and will not absorb, here's what to do.

• Soak them in the washer in cold water and ¼ cup of Epsom salts overnight. Add detergent and wash as usual.

• Wash nonabsorbent towels several times in a row and do not add fabric softener.

• Sometimes hanging these towels to dry instead of drying in the dryer for a couple of washings works well.

Do not wash anything else with towels. Washing things together transfers lint from item to item. Always wash towels in the hottest possible water.

If your towels have a mildew odor, sprinkle them lightly with ODORZOUT™ and let sit for a day or so, then dump into the washer (towels and ODORZOUT™) and launder as usual.

㉟ Window Treatments

Be sure to read the care label and closely follow instructions when you are cleaning your drapes and curtains. Never try to wash curtains that should be dry-cleaned.

You can extend the life of window coverings by vacuuming them frequently with the upholstery attachments on your vacuum cleaner. You may also take them down and shake them, or tumble them in the dryer on the air setting.

Do not allow draperies to become heavily soiled before cleaning, especially if they are labeled "dry clean only."

Dry cleaning does not clean as well as wet cleaning, and all soil may not be removed.

Sunlight weakens and damages fiber and color. If the curtains or drapes are covering a particularly sunny window, hanging a blind or shade to protect the fabric might be a wise idea.

Remove all hooks, etc., from curtains prior to washing. Follow the directions for the type of fabric on the care label directions.

Some curtains can be dried in the dryer. Check the care label. Just be sure not to overcrowd the dryer, and remember to rearrange the draperies often during the drying cycle.

If pressing is required, remove the curtains while damp and iron. This will make it easier to remove the wrinkles. For a crisp finish, use spray sizing or starch. Remember, two light sprays are better than one heavy one and will prevent white "flaking" on the fabric.

Sizing and starch will help to repel dirt as well.

If you've washed sheer or lace-type curtains, pressing them gently while damp and hanging them slightly damp will encourage them to fall into gentle folds at the window.

Plastic shower curtains: Wash these in the washing machine with several old, light colored towels. Add 1½ cups of white vinegar and your normal detergent, fill with warm water, and use the gentle cycle. Remove the curtain promptly from the washer and hang immediately. This method will remove soap scum and dirt. If mold and mildew are a problem, use 1½ cups of liquid chlorine bleach instead of white vinegar and follow the above directions.

Bedtime

We're going to wash those pillows, sheets, blankets and comforters. No sleeping on the job!

Pillows

To freshen pillows, tumble them in the clothes dryer set on air or warm for 30 minutes with several barely damp light-colored towels and a dryer fabric softener sheet. Don't use the fabric softener sheet if you have fragrance allergies.

Fiber-filled pillows: These flatten with use, so chances are you'll want to restore their bulk and softness. Clean them in your washing machine every couple of months, and choose a windy day if possible. Wash the pillows in cold or lukewarm water with a mild detergent, and use a short cycle. If you have allergies, try Fresh Breeze Laundry Soap™ by Soapworks. Make sure the pillows are rinsed well, then spin them dry.

If you are washing pillows by hand, use cool water and mild suds, and press out all the water you can. Rinse several times to remove all the soap, then press and roll out the water.

Hang pillows to dry in a shady, breezy location if possible, turning them frequently. Finally, place pillows in the dryer on the lowest setting to fluff the filling. Adding a new tennis ball or clean tennis shoe in the dryer will help to pump up the volume!

Place pillows inside zippered pillow covers to keep them clean and fresh longer.

Feather pillows: Wash these in cool suds and dry them in the shade. Heat can release traces of oil in the feathers and cause them to give off unpleasant odors.

Make sure you allow plenty of time for the feathers to dry. Fluff and shake the pillow frequently to rearrange the feathers for better drying.

You may put feather pillows in the dryer on the air setting to reposition the feathers and add bounce to the pillows. Again, putting in a couple of tennis balls or clean tennis shoes will beat the feathers up and add fluff. Keeping feather pillows in zippered pillow protectors is also a good idea.

Other pillows: There are a lot of different pillows on the market these days, including specially formed cervical pillows. Wash them according to the care label so you don't damage the filling.

Sheets

Always wash sheets before using them for the first time.

Mend tears before laundering or they will become huge holes.

Wash dark sheets separately from white or light colors to avoid color runs.

Use warm water for polyester and blends. Use hot water for 100 percent cotton sheets. Dry according to care label directions, usually on medium.

Flannel Sheets and Pillowcases

Launder these in the washing machine with warm water, and always make sure to wash them before using for the first time. Bear in mind that flannel sheets have an enormous amount of lint, so they may not be suitable for people with allergies (although the more they are laundered the less severe the lint will be). Rinse with warm water and a cup of white vinegar to help with the lint problem, and make sure you clean the lint filter frequently during the drying cycle the first few times you wash and dry the sheets. Wash flannel separately from all other fabrics.

Blankets

If the care label indicates that your blankets are machine washable, which most are, make sure the machine has plenty of room for movement between the folds of the blanket. Wash with mild soap in cold water and add 1 cup of white vinegar to the final rinse to remove any soap residue and keep the blankets soft. If the care tag indicates, dry in a warm dryer or out of direct sunlight over several clotheslines strung at least 12 inches apart to avoid stretching the blanket. Store blankets well by wrapping them in plastic, or inside a clean pillowcase.

For electric blankets or mattress pads, follow the care label directions carefully to avoid damaging the wiring and creating a possible fire hazard.

Bedspreads

Washable spreads should be laundered according to the care label directions. Nylon, polyester, polyester blends and cotton bedspreads all wash well. Rayons, silks and acetates should be dry-cleaned.

Chenille spreads, which are quite popular again, are easily laundered in the washing machine. Use warm water and mild detergent and rinse well. Dry in the dryer and shake well to restore the nap when you remove chenille from the dryer. Linting, which is common in these types of spreads, will stop after a few washings. Be sure to keep your dryer's lint filter well cleaned when drying these spreads.

For heavily quilted spreads you can use tennis balls or a clean tennis shoe to pump up the volume on the quilting.

Down Comforters

I find that it's best—and also easiest—to have these cleaned professionally. If you do decide to launder yours, use a commercial-size washer, using the shortest possible cycle.

Do not wash these more frequently than you have to. Air the comforter frequently instead, and use a duvet cover or comforter cover that can be laundered as needed.

Feather Beds

Follow the directions that come with your feather bed and accessories. Be sure to read all of the cleaning information and follow care instructions carefully.

Mattresses

It's important to turn your mattress every three months to allow for even wear. Alternate between turning it end to end and side to side.

Covering a mattress with a pad or a plastic zip mattress protector is your best defense against stains, especially on a child's bed. A cloth pad is much cooler than plastic.

If you are faced with cleaning up a wet spill, such as urine, absorb all the moisture you can with paper towels or rags, applying pressure as you blot. Clean the area with Spot Shot Instant Carpet Stain Remover® and stand the mattress on its side against a wall to speed drying and keep moisture from going deeper into the mattress. Once the mattress is dry, apply a layer of ODORZOUT™ to absorb the odor. ODORZOUT™ is an odor eliminator, not a cover-up. If you can lay the mattress out in the sun to dry, it will speed up the process.

37

Preserving Your Wedding Gown

Wedding gowns are expensive investments, but with so much excitement leading up to the big day, cleaning the dress afterward rarely crosses our minds. Often the dress is quickly discarded in favor of more comfortable travel attire, then it's left to lay while we trip off on our honeymoon. Yet, with just a little bit of care you can preserve the dress, for sentimental reasons perhaps, or for your own daughter to wear someday. Here's what you need to know.

First, don't leave the store without a care label. If a care label is not sewn into the gown, be sure to get written cleaning instructions from the store clerk or seamstress.

Once you have chosen your gown, it's best to leave it at the store until the last possible moment. You'll avoid wrinkling that way. If you bring your dress home prior to the big day, decide where you are going to hang it to avoid wrinkling— perhaps an over-the-door hanger in a spare room. Do not hang your precious dress in the attic or the basement. You'll only be inviting dust, dirt, bugs, dampness, and water damage.

Now what about after the wedding? Don't just throw your dress down. Hang it on a padded hanger. Assign some- one to pick up the dress within a day or two after the wed- ding and transport it to the cleaner you have chosen. Those spots and spills and lipstick smudges from all those happy kisses will come out much more easily if you have the dress cleaned sooner, *not* later. Ask your mom, sister, or best friend to help out. Whatever you do, don't come home from your honeymoon to a dirty dress laying in a pile on the floor. Even if it never is worn again, you can have beautiful pillows made from the fabric and veiling to use on a bed. That's what I did!

Always have the dress professionally cleaned *before* you put it into storage. Your dress may have invisible stains from food, beverages, perfume, and body oil. If these stains are not properly cleaned, they can become permanent. Try to point out stains or spills to your cleaner *before* cleaning.

A lot of wedding gowns are beaded or lavishly trimmed. Inspect these trims with your cleaner prior to cleaning, since many of them are not made to withstand the dry-cleaning process. Beads, glitter, and pearls are made of coated plastic and may be attached to the dress with adhesives that will not weather cleaning chemicals. Some trims may yellow during the process. Some items "dyed to match" may not be color- fast and may not match after cleaning.

Look for a qualified, experienced cleaner in your area who will discuss all of these things with you and closely examine your dress for potential problems.

Storing Your Gown

Sadly, no cleaning process or storage method can guarantee against yellowing and deterioration of the fabric in your gown. There are, however, steps that you can take to ensure the best possible results.

• Have your dress packed in a special heirloom storage box. You can have your cleaner pack the dress, or buy the box and pack it yourself. Remember to use non-acid tissue paper.

• Wrap the dress in a sheet if it is not boxed. Do not store in plastic or it will yellow.

• Stuff the bodice and sleeves with white, non-acid tissue paper to prevent permanent wrinkles.

• Store headpieces, veils, shoes and other accessories separately. A box or bag will be fine. No plastic, though.

• Store in a cool, dry place. The basement and the attic, though popular, are not good choices.

• If you decide to store your dress on a hanger, hanging it from the sewn-in straps will prevent damage to the shoulders.

• Look your gown over once a year—Valentine's Day is a memorable date—to ensure that no spots have been overlooked. If you find any spotting or discoloration, have the dress treated by a professional cleaner as soon as possible.

Follow these tips and your wedding gown will have a happy future.

38
Cleaning Guide for Fabric Types

I am the "stain stalker," and in these next pages I am going to walk you through laundry procedures for certain fabric types and unusual items.

Acetate: This is a temperamental fabric. Do not allow it to become heavily soiled and do not use an enzyme detergent when laundering. Acetate is commonly used for curtains, brocades, taffetas, and satin. (Think evening wear.) It's also a popular lining. You can machine wash acetate in cold water or you can hand wash. Be sure not to spin or wring acetate as this will set wrinkles. Rinse extremely well and press with a cool (low setting) iron on the wrong side of the fabric.

Acrylic: This fabric should be laundered frequently since it can retain perspiration odors. Acrylic is usually machine washable in cool water. Check the care label. Dry flat or hang to dry, being sure to reshape the garment while it is still damp.

Angora: This wool is made from rabbit fur or goat hair. Angora sheds a lot, although if it's blended with nylon it will shed less. Wash angora in warm or cool water using a very mild soap or a little shampoo. Do not rub, twist, or lift the garment up and down in the water as this will cause stretching. Washing in a sink is best. Let the water run out and then press the liquid out of the garment. Rinse well again, pressing the water out. Roll the garment in a towel and then reshape. Dry flat out of the sun. Do not press—instead, hold a steam iron just above the garment to remove wrinkles.

Blends: Blends, such as cotton/polyester, are made from combined fibers. To launder these fabrics, follow the guidelines for the most delicate or the most prominent fiber. The most common blends are cotton/polyester, cotton/linen, and silk/polyester.

Brocades: Use care when laundering brocades. You don't want to crush or flatten the pile design. Hand wash in cool water or dry clean according to the care label. Do not wring. Iron on the "wrong" side using a press cloth or towel between the fabric and the iron.

Canvas: A heavy, firm, very tightly woven fabric, canvas was originally made from cotton or linen, but now it comes in synthetics or blends. Machine wash canvas in cold water and tumble dry on a low setting. Test for colorfastness before washing. If it's not colorfast, have it dry-cleaned.

Cashmere: This is an expensive fiber that comes from the undercoat of cashmere goats. Treat it with respect. Dry clean these prizes or hand wash with care in cool water and well-dissolved gentle soap. Rinse well and do not wring. Dry flat, reshaping the garment as it dries. Iron on the "wrong" side while still damp with a cool iron, if necessary.

Chiffon: This is a very thin, transparent fabric, made from silk or synthetic fibers. Hand wash as you would silk.

Chintz: Glazed cotton, and often printed. Dry clean this fabric unless the label states that it can be washed. Follow the care label instructions carefully.

Corduroy: Take care when washing corduroy. It wears well, but care is needed to avoid crushing and distorting the pile. Turn corduroy inside out and launder using warm water. Dry at a normal setting. Remove from the dryer while still damp and smooth the seams, pockets, etc. Hang to complete drying, and iron on the "wrong" side of the fabric. Pile may be restored by brushing gently.

Cotton: This natural vegetable fiber is woven and knitted into fabrics in all weights and textures. Hand wash light-weight fabrics such as organdy and batiste and hang to air dry. Iron when damp with a hot iron.

Machine wash light-colored and white medium to heavy-weight cottons in warm water. Use cold water for bright colors that may bleed. Dry on a low dryer setting. Remove from the dryer while still damp and iron with a hot iron right away.

Damask: This is a jacquard-weave fabric. It may be made of cotton, linen, silk, wool, or a blend. Hand wash lightweight fabrics and be sure to check the individual fiber listings. Dry clean silk, wool and all heavier weight fabrics.

Denim: If you have jeans, you know this strong fabric is prone to shrinking, streaking and fading. Machine wash denim in warm water. Blue and other deep colors bleed the first several washings, so be sure to wash separately. Washing older, faded jeans with the new ones will restore some of their original color. Dry at low settings to avoid shrinkage. Iron while damp if necessary and be aware that jeans may bleed color onto your ironing board.

Down: Down is the soft underfeather of waterfowl that is often combined with adult feathers. It is machine washable *and* dry-cleanable. Just be sure to follow the care label closely. Much of the treatment will depend on the fabric covering the down, so pay attention to manufacturer's directions.

Do not air-dry down. It dries too slowly and mold or mildew may form in the process. Dry in your dryer, using a large capacity dryer if need be. Set temperatures low (under 140 degrees), fluffing and turning the item often. Make sure to dry the item thoroughly. This can take time.

Want really fluffy duvets and pillows? Putting a clean tennis shoe or tennis ball in with the item will fluff it up!

Flannel: Flannel is actually a napped fabric, and it comes in a plain or twill-type weave. Cotton and synthetics should be washed according to the care label, but when in doubt, use cool water and mild detergent. Dry at a low dryer setting and remove flannel while damp to avoid wrinkles. You may also line-dry this fabric. Wool flannel should be dry-cleaned.

Gabardine: Firm, tightly woven twill fabric, often worsted wool, but sometimes made of cotton and synthetic fibers. We are seeing a large amount of synthetic fibers sold as gabardine in trousers and blazers for men and women. Follow your label directions—many synthetics are machine washable and dryable. If the care label says dry clean, be sure to do so.

Lace: An extremely delicate fabric, lace may be made of cotton, linen or synthetic. Wash using a mild soap or detergent intended for delicates. Avoid rubbing since it will distort the fibers. Rinse well without wringing, shape by hand, and hang to air-dry or dry flat. Delicate lace pieces may need to be reshaped and pinned down to dry. If you must iron lace, do so over a terrycloth towel. (White is best.) Never put lace in the dryer.

Leather and suede: Generally, leather and suede are not washable. Check your care label carefully. If you have washable leather items, wash them by hand and be sure to protect them with a leather spray protectant. To clean suede, rub it with another piece of suede or a suede brush (not any other kind of brush) to restore the nap and keep it looking new.

Remember, leather needs to breathe, so do not cover it with plastic or store in a tightly enclosed area. If you are looking for a dust cover for leather or suede, use cloth—an old pillowcase is ideal.

To remove spots from leather (not for suede), try using cuticle remover. Rub it into the spot, wait 10 minutes, and then massage the area with a cloth dipped in the cuticle remover. Wipe down thoroughly.

To remove spots from suede, try dabbing with white vinegar.

Linen: A tough fabric that withstands high temperatures, linen is a favorite in hot climates. It is made of natural flax fiber, and comes in light to heavyweight fabrics. Hand wash or machine wash linen in warm water (again, read your care label). If the fabric is colorfast you may remove stains and brighten the fabric with an oxygen bleach or Brilliant Bleach™ from Soapworks. Do not use chlorine bleach.

Iron while still damp, and to help prevent creasing you may treat with starch or sizing. Press heavyweight linens with a hot iron, and for lighter weight linen and blends (linen, plus other fibers), iron with a warm iron.

Linen is also dry-cleanable.

Mohair: An oldie but a goodie! This is fiber taken from angora goats. Follow the directions for cleaning wool.

Nylon: This is a durable synthetic fiber that comes in varying weights and is often blended with other fibers. When used alone it is machine washable in warm water. It can also be cleaned.

Dry on a low setting or hang to dry using a nonmetal hanger. Do not dry in sunlight—that will cause yellowing. Nonchlorine bleach is best for nylon

Organdy: Think party dress! Sheer and lightweight, organdy is actually a cotton fiber. Hand wash this and iron damp with a hot iron. Use starch as you iron to give it a crisp look. May also be dry-cleaned.

Polyester: This strong synthetic fiber won't stretch or shrink, which is probably why it's so popular. It comes in various weights and textures, and is often found blended with cotton and wool.

Wash polyester in warm water. Tumble dry and make sure not to let it sit in the dryer, because that will encourage wrinkles. Remove it immediately and you may not need to iron it. If ironing *is* necessary, make sure to use a low setting.

If the polyester is blended with another fiber, just follow the washing instructions for the more delicate fiber.

Ramie: Very similar to linen, ramie is a natural fiber made from—what else—the ramie plant! It can be used alone or blended with other fibers, such as ramie/cotton.

Machine wash in warm water, tumble dry and iron while damp with a hot iron. Avoid twisting the fibers or they will become distorted. May be dry-cleaned also.

Rayon: This is a synthetic fiber that is sometimes called "viscose." Follow the care label directions closely, but for the very best results, have this fabric dry-cleaned. Dry-cleaning not only cleans well, but it gives rayon the crisp pressing it needs to maintain its shape and good looks.

Satin: Originally made only from silk, this shiny fabric is available in acetate, cotton, nylon, and even polyester.

Dry clean satin made out of silk and acetate. You may wash cotton, nylon and polyester satins, as long as you follow the washing instructions for those fibers.

Seersucker: You've seen this fabric in shirts, blouses and nightwear. It has puckered stripes that are woven in during the manufacturing process. Seersucker is most frequently made of cotton, but it's also available in nylon and polyester. Be guided by the fiber content for washing and drying.

Drip-dry or tumble dry and iron on low heat if necessary.

Silk: This is a natural fiber made by the silkworm. It is a delicate fabric that requires special care to avoid damage. Check the care labels, but you may be able to hand wash crepe de chine, thin, lightweight and medium weight silk in lukewarm water with mild soap or detergent. You can also use cold water with cold water detergent.

Do not use chlorine bleach. You may use Brilliant Bleach™ by Soapworks without damaging the fibers.

Rinsing silk well is important. Rinse several times in cold water to remove all suds. Towel blot and dry flat. Do not wring or rub silk.

Iron on the "wrong" side of the fabric with a warm iron.

If your care label indicates that the garment is machine washable, follow the directions with the utmost care. Dry cleaning works best for suits, pleated silks, and silks that are not colorfast.

Do not use strong spotters or enzyme spotters on silk.

Spandex: Spandex is added to other fibers to give them stretch and elasticity. Machine wash in warm water on the delicate or gentle cycle. Do not use chlorine bleach. Do not put them in the dryer, or iron, high heat will break down spandex fibers. Line dry or dry flat, per care label.

If you have exercise clothes containing spandex, be sure to launder each time you wear them. Body oil can break down spandex fibers.

Terry cloth: A toweling-type of fabric, terry cloth has a looped pile made of cotton or cotton/polyester blend. You find it in towels, of course, and even sleepwear.

Machine wash in warm or hot water. Tumble or line dry. Add softener for a softer texture.

Velour: This is a napped fabric that is available in wool, cotton, silk and synthetics. Dry clean unless the care label indicates it can be washed and dried.

Velvet: A beautiful soft pile fabric, velvet comes in silk, rayon or cotton. Dry clean for best results.

To raise the pile on velvet, steam from the "wrong" side over a pot of boiling water. Hold the fabric at least 12 inches from the water, and be careful not to allow the fabric to come in contact with the water. This works well for creases in the back of dresses, etc.

Wool: This is a natural fiber made from the fleece of sheep. Hand wash sweaters and other knits in cold water with cold water detergent. Rinse several times and do not wring or twist.

Towel blot and dry flat, reshaping as needed.

A to Z Palace Spot and Stain Removal Guide

I'm so glad that you feel safe in airing your dirty laundry with me. I am, after all, the Babe of Borax, one of the original Mold-Diggers, the High Priestess of Household Chemicals, the Vixen of Vinegar, the Deaconess of Dry Cleaning, the Goddess of Grease Stains, the Sultaness of Soap, Solvents and Solutions and of course, the Queen of Clean®! And you know what else? I'm not finished yet . . . not until I give you this, my "all you need to know" spot and stain removal guide, straight from the palace!

Now, a few words of caution before we begin. *Don't* go trying any of these spot removal methods *without* paying heed to my Royal Rules of Stain Removal. Promise?

Royal Rules of Stain Removal

• Test the spot remover on hidden or inconspicuous areas of the fabric before you proceed.

• Approach the stain from the wrong side of the fabric.

Put a pad of paper toweling under the offending spot as you work. This will help to blot the stain.

• Always blot, never rub! Rubbing will spread the spot and harm the fabric.

• Do not iron or apply heat to spots or stains. Heat will set the stain and you will never be able to remove it.

• If you don't know what caused the stain, start with the weakest and simplest stain removal method.

• Make sure to consider the fabric as well as the stain.

• Remember, the faster you react to a spill or a spot, the better your chances are of removing it completely.

• Directing a blow-dryer at a freshly blotted spot will help it to dry without a ring.

• Sometimes you may still need to pretreat using your favorite laundry spotter, such as Zout™.

A to Z

ACID: Acid can permanently damage fabrics, so it must be treated immediately. Neutralize acid by flushing the area with cold running water as soon as possible. Next, spread the garment over a pad of paper towels and moisten with ammonia. Dab the spot several times, then flush again with cold water. If you do not have ammonia on hand, apply a paste of cold water and baking soda, then flush with water. Repeat this several times, then launder as usual.

Do not use undiluted ammonia on wool or silk, or on any blends containing these fibers. If you have acid on silk or wool you may dilute ammonia with equal parts of cold water and apply as directed above.

ADHESIVE TAPE: Sponge adhesive tape with eucalyptus oil, baby oil, or cooking oil. Allow to soak 10 minutes or so, then work in undiluted dishwashing liquid and rinse well. Pretreat and launder as usual.

You may also consider using De-Solv-it™, Goo Gone™, or Un-Du™ to remove adhesives from fabric and hard surfaces. Un-Du™ is so great it will remove a stamp from an envelope!

ALCOHOLIC BEVERAGES: These stains will turn brown with age, so it is important to treat them as soon as possible. First, flush the area with cold water or with club soda, then sponge immediately with a cloth barely dampened with warm water and 1 or 2 drops of liquid dish soap. Rinse with cool water and dry the area with a hair dryer set on medium.

Alcohol is often invisible when it is spilled, but it can oxidize with heat and age, which makes it impossible to remove. Presoak dry alcohol stains in an enzyme solution such as Biz All Fabric Bleach™, and launder as usual.

If you spill alcohol on a dry-clean-only fabric, sponge with cold water or club soda and then take the garment to the dry cleaner as soon as possible. Make sure to point out the stain.

For beer spills, sponge with a solution of equal parts white vinegar and dishwashing liquid, then rinse in warm water.

For treating red and white wine spills, see **Wine.**

ANIMAL HAIR: Removing pet hair from clothes and bedding can be a challenge. Try using a damp sponge and wiping over clothes and bedding, etc. Rinse the sponge frequently to keep it clean. You can also remove hair by putting on rubber gloves and dipping them in water. Simply dip and wipe, dip and wipe. The hair will rinse off easily.

ANTIPERSPIRANTS AND DEODORANTS: Antiperspirants that contain aluminum chloride are acidic and may interact with some fabrics. If color changes have occurred, try sponging fabric with ammonia. Rinse thoroughly, and remember to dilute ammonia with equal portions of water when spotting wool or silk.

If you want to avoid yellow underarm stains and prevent color removal, take a bar of Fels-Naptha Soap® and work it into the underarm of clothes *before* you launder them for the first time, even if you see no visible stain. Work up a good lather between your thumbs and then launder as usual.

You can also try applying rubbing alcohol to the stain and covering the area with a folded paper towel dampened with alcohol. Keep it moist and let it sit for a few hours prior to laundering.

To treat yellowed areas that have become stiff, apply an enzyme-soaking product. Biz All Fabric Bleach™ is a good one to try. Make a stiff paste of the powder by mixing it with cold water. Rub it into the stained areas. Next, put the garment in a plastic bag and leave 8 hours or overnight. Wash in very hot water. If dealing with fabrics that can't withstand hot water, drape the underarm area over a sink and pour 1 quart of hot water through the fabric. Launder as usual.

Don't iron over a deodorant stain or you will never be able to remove it.

I have also had success soaking garments with underarm stains in a solution of 1 quart warm water and 3 tablespoons of Brilliant Bleach™. Soak up to several days if necessary. Brilliant Bleach™ is safe for whites and colorfast garments.

Last-ditch effort: Spray the stained area heavily with heated white vinegar, work in Twenty Mule Team Borax™, roll up in a plastic bag and leave overnight, then launder as usual.

BABY FORMULA: For white clothes, try applying lemon juice to the stains and laying the garment in the sun. Pretreat and launder as usual.

Unseasoned meat tenderizer is also great for removing formula and baby food stains. Make a paste of the tenderizer and cool water, rub it into the stain and let sit for an hour or so before laundering. Meat tenderizer contains an enzyme that breaks down protein stains. Just make sure to use *unseasoned* tenderizer.

Soaking colored clothes and whites in Brilliant Bleach™ is also effective, although you may have to soak for several days to achieve perfect results on difficult stains. Remember, this bleach is nonchlorine, so it's totally safe for baby things.

BARBEQUE SAUCE: See *Tomato-Based Stains.*

BERRIES (blueberries, cranberries, raspberries, strawberries): There are many complex ways to deal with berry stains, but I've had great success with one of the simplest, a product called Wine Away Red Wine Stain Remover™. Don't be fooled by the name, it works on red fruit stains and juices too.

Just spray Wine Away™ straight on the fabric and watch in amazement as it breaks down the stain. Follow the directions on the container carefully and launder immediately after use. Totally nontoxic, Wine Away™ is safe on all washable surfaces.

BEVERAGES: Blot beverage spills immediately until you have absorbed all you can, then sponge with clean, warm water and a little borax. (About ½ teaspoon Borax to ½ cup of water.) Sponge and blot repeatedly and launder as usual.

Also see information under specific beverage stains.

BLOOD (fresh and dried): If you have blood all over your clothes, laundry may not be your biggest problem . . . for those little accidents try the following:

For washable fabrics, soak as soon as possible in salt water or flush with club soda. You can also make a paste of unseasoned meat tenderizer and cold water, and apply it to the stain for a few hours. Wash in cool water and detergent, by hand or machine.

Pouring 3 percent hydrogen peroxide through the stained area can be effective in many instances. The sooner you do this the more success you will have. Make sure to do this only on washable fabrics, please. Pour the peroxide through the stain, then flush with cold water, pretreat and launder as usual.

Biz All Fabric Bleach™ and Brilliant Bleach™ both work well on blood. When using Biz™, make a paste with cold water and apply to the stain, allowing it to sit for several hours. With Brilliant Bleach™, soak the garment for a significant period of time—anywhere between 1 to 24 hours. Neither of these products will harm colorfast fabrics.

For dry-clean-only fabrics, sprinkle with salt while the blood is still moist, then take to a dry cleaner as soon as possible.

Human saliva will break down fresh bloodstains, so try applying a little of your own saliva to a small spot of blood—this may do the trick.

For a quick fix for fresh bloodstains, apply cornstarch to the surface and then flush from the wrong side of the fabric with soapy water. Pretreat and launder as usual.

Blood on leather can be foamed away with 3 percent hydrogen peroxide. Dab on the peroxide. Let it bubble and then blot. Continue until the blood is removed. Wipe the surface with a damp cloth and dry.

BUTTER OR MARGARINE: Scrape off any solid concentration of butter with a dull edge, such as the back of a knife. On washable fabrics, work in undiluted dishwashing liquid, wash and dry.

If the stain is old, spray it with WD-40 Lubricant® to regenerate the grease, then work in undiluted dishwashing liquid and wash in the hottest water possible for that fabric type.

Sponge silks and delicate fabrics with Energine Cleaning Fluid™. Allow to air-dry. Repeat if necessary.

Do not iron the fabric until all traces of the grease have been removed. Ironing will set the stain and make it impossible to remove.

Take dry-clean-only fabrics to the dry cleaner as soon as possible. Be sure to identify the stain and its location on the garment.

CANDLE WAX: For candle wax on clothes and table linens, place the article in a plastic bag, place the bag in the freezer and let the wax freeze. Scrape off what you can with a dull, straight edge—the back of a knife or an old credit card works well. Lay a brown paper bag, with no writing facing the fabric, on the ironing board. (Grocery store bags work well. Just make sure that the writing is face down on the ironing board *away* from the fabric—otherwise you may transfer lettering to your garment.) Cover with a similar bag (again, with the writing *away* from the fabric) and press with a medium/hot iron, moving the paper bag like a blotter until you have absorbed every bit of wax you can. Be patient! Blot with Energine Cleaning Fluid® to remove the balance of the grease from the wax.

Wieman Wax Away™ also works beautifully on any kind of wax. Follow the directions with care.

CANDY: To remove candy from fabrics, combine 1 table-spoon of liquid dish soap with 1 tablespoon of white vinegar and 1 quart of warm water. Soak the stain in it for 15 to 30 minutes, then flush with warm, clear water. Pretreat and launder as usual.

For chocolate stains, see **Chocolate.**

CHEWING GUM: See **Gum.**

CHOCOLATE: Scrape off all that you can, then soak washable fabrics for 30 minutes in an enzyme prewash solution such as Biz™. Rub detergent into any remaining stain and work well between your thumbs. Rinse the area under forcefully running cold water. If a grease spot remains, sponge the area with dry-cleaning solution such as Energine Cleaning Fluid®. Any residual stain should come out during normal washing. If the stain is still visible after washing, soak in Brilliant Bleach™ or combine ½ cup of 3 percent hydrogen peroxide and 1 teaspoon of clear ammonia and soak the stain for 10 minutes at a time, checking every 10 minutes and resoaking if necessary. Remember, fabrics need to be tested for colorfastness before using peroxide.

For dry-clean-only fabrics, flush the stain with club soda to prevent setting, then sponge the area with Energine Cleaning Fluid®. If the stain persists, take it to your dry cleaner.

COFFEE AND TEA (black or with sugar): Blot up all that you can and, if the garment is washable, flush immediately with cold water. Rub detergent into the stain and work well between your thumbs before laundering as usual. If the stain is still visible and you can use hot water on the fabric, spread the stain over the sink, or stretch over a bowl and tie or rubber band in place (like a little trampoline) and sit the bowl in the sink. Cover the stain with Twenty Mule Team Borax™ and pour boiling water through it, circling from the outside of the stain until you have reached the center. Let soak 30 minutes to an hour and relaunder.

For more delicate fabrics, soak in Brilliant Bleach™.

For sturdy whites, such as knits and T-shirts, dissolve 2 denture-cleaning tablets in warm water and soak the stain for 30 minutes. Check the garment. If the stain is still visible, soak again and launder as usual.

Out at a restaurant? Dip your napkin in water and sprinkle with salt and blot the offending stain.

For stains from lattes and cappuccinos, see **Milk.**

COLA AND SOFT DRINKS: Sponge these spills as soon as possible with a solution of equal parts alcohol and water. On washable clothes, bleach out remaining stains with an equal mixture of 3 percent hydrogen peroxide and water. Saturate stain and wait 20 minutes. If the stain is gone, launder as usual. Repeat if the stain remains. You can also soak the fabric in a solution of Brilliant Bleach™ as directed on the container.

Borax is also effective in soft drink/cola removal. Moisten the spot thoroughly and sprinkle with borax, working well between your thumbs. Flush with water and re-treat if necessary.

Getting the stain out as soon as possible is important: cola and soft drinks will discolor fabrics as they oxidize.

COLLAR STAINS: This is for those women whose husbands won't share laundry duty, the women who didn't know that the wedding ring came with a ring around the collar! It's easy to remove, though. Just use some inexpensive shampoo! Shampoo dissolves body oils so it works great on that collar ring. Keep some in a bottle with a dispenser top in the laundry room. Squirt on enough to cover the offending stain and work it in well, then launder as usual.

COPIER TONER (powder): First, carefully shake off any loose powder and brush lightly with a soft brush. An old, soft toothbrush works well. Pretreat with your favorite spotter or try Zout™ or Spot Shot Instant Carpet Stain Remover® and launder as usual, using the hottest water for the fabric type. Don't rub or brush with your hand. The oil in your skin will spread and set the stain.

COSMETICS (foundation, blusher, eye shadow, eyeliner, and mascara): Bar soap such as Dove®, Caress™ and other such beauty bars work well on cosmetics spots. Wet the stain and rub with the soap, working it in well. Flush with warm water and, once stain is removed, launder as usual.

Sometimes just working in laundry detergent will be all you need. For difficult cases, add some borax to the area and work well between your thumbs.

If your garment is dry clean only, try some Energine Cleaning Fluid® directly on the spot. Make sure to use a cool blow-dryer to keep a ring from forming on the fabric. You'll need to take the garment to a professional cleaner if the stain doesn't come out. (See also *Makeup.*)

CRAYON AND COLORED PENCIL: Place the stained area on a pad of paper towels and spray with WD-40 Lubricant®. Let stand for a few minutes, then turn the fabric over and spray the other side. Let sit for a further 10 minutes before working undiluted dishwashing liquid into the stained area to remove the crayon and oil. Replace the paper-toweling pad as necessary. Wash in the hottest possible water for the fabric, along with your normal detergent and appropriate bleaching agent (depending on whether the clothes are white or colored). Wash on the longest wash cycle available, and rinse well.

Another way to remove crayon from washable fabrics such as wool, acrylic, linen, cotton and polyester, is to lay the offending stain between two pieces of brown paper and press with a warm/medium iron. A grocery bag works well—just remember to keep any ink that may be on the bag away from the fabric. The paper works as a blotter to absorb the crayon, so keep changing it as the wax is absorbed. If any color mark remains, soak the garment in Brilliant Bleach™ or flush with Energine Cleaning Fluid®.

Note: Don't panic if the crayon has also gone through the dryer. Simply spray an old rag with WD-40 Lubricant®, then thoroughly wipe down the drum. Make sure the dryer is empty when you do this—no clothes, no crayons. Place a load of dry rags in the dryer and run through a drying cycle when you're through. This will remove any oily residue.

DYE (see also **Hair Dye):** Dye stains are difficult if not impossible to remove. Try one or all of these methods.

Spread the stained area over a bowl and put a rubber band around the fabric *and* the bowl to hold the fabric taut, like a trampoline. Sit the bowl in the sink with the drain in the open position to allow the water to run freely away. Turn on the cold water faucet to a nice steady drip and let it drip through the dye spot for 3 to 6 hours. Monitor the sink to be sure the water is draining. This treatment is effective in many cases.

You can also try saturating the dye spot with a combination of equal parts 3 percent hydrogen peroxide and water. Sit the fabric in the sun, keeping it moist with the solution until the spot completely disappears. Rinse well and launder as usual. Use only on colorfast clothes.

If your dye problem is caused from fugitive color—that is, color that has run from one fabric to another during the wash cycle—all the bleaching in the world won't help. Try Synthrapol™ or Carbona Color Run Remover™ instead.

Quilters have used Synthrapol™ for years to remove color that runs in homemade quilts. Make sure to read *all* the directions on the bottle prior to using.

Carbona Color Run Remover™ is extremely effective on cotton fabrics. It is not for delicates or some blends, so do read the box with care. It may also cause damage to buttons and, in some cases, zippers. You may want to remove these prior to treating.

EGG: First scrape off any solid matter. Then, soak the fabric in a glass or plastic container with any enzyme-soaking product, such as Biz Non Chlorine Bleach™. Soak for at least 6 hours or overnight. If a stain remains, work in powder detergent, rubbing vigorously between your thumbs. Rinse and wash as usual. Check the garment carefully for any remaining stain when you remove it from the washer. Don't apply heat until all of the stain is removed or the stain will become permanent.

You can also try treating the area with cool water and unseasoned meat tenderizer. Work this into the area well, and allow it to sit for a few hours, being sure to keep the area moist. Continue treating until no stain remains.

Take nonwashables to the dry cleaner as soon as possible. Quick treatment is important. Make sure you identify the stain to your cleaner so it can be treated properly and promptly.

EYELINER AND EYE SHADOW: See *Cosmetics.*

FABRIC SOFTENER SPOTS: For the greasy spots that sometimes appear on clothes after drying with dryer fabric softcner sheets, dampen the spot and rub with pure bar soap and relaunder.

For spots from liquid fabric softener, rub with undiluted liquid dish soap and relaunder.

FELT TIP MARKER: See *Marker.*

FOOD DYE: Fruit juices, gelatin desserts, fruit smoothies, and frozen fruit sticks all contain food dye that can leave a nasty stain on clothes.

Treating the stain while it is still fresh is the very best thing you can do. If you are out in public and don't have access to any cleaning supplies, wet the spot with club soda or cool water and blot, blot, blot. If you are at home, then treat the spot with 1 cup of cool water to which you have added 1 tablespoon of ammonia. Once you have flushed the spot well with this solution, grab the salt shaker and rub salt into the wound . . . I mean stain! Let this sit for an hour or so, and then brush off the salt. If the stain is still visible, re-treat the same way.

You can also try stretching the fabric tight and holding it under a forceful stream of cold water. This will flush out much of the spot without spreading it. Next, rub in your favorite detergent, scrubbing vigorously between your thumbs. Rinse again in cool water. Do not apply heat to the stain until it is completely removed.

I have had great success soaking food dye spills in Brilliant Bleach™ (follow the directions for hand-soaking on the container).

If you are dealing with a red, orange, or purple stain, try Wine Away Red Wine Stain Remover™, used according to directions. Don't be fooled by the name—it is great for all red-type stains. You will be amazed!

Remember, if the stain is not removed during the spotting process, it will not come out in the laundry!

FRUIT AND FRUIT JUICE (also see *Berries*): These stains absolutely must be removed before the fabric is washed. The combination of heat and age will set fruit stains and they will be impossible to remove, even for the Queen.

Sponge or spray the area immediately with soda water or seltzer. If these products aren't available, use cold water. *Do not use hot water.* Rinse the offending spot as soon as possible while it is still wet. Rub in your favorite detergent and scrub the area between your thumbs. *Now* rinse under hot running water—as hot as the fabric can tolerate. Pull the fabric taut and allow the full force of the water to flow through the area. The stronger the flow the better.

If the stain is still visible after this treatment, make a paste of Twenty Mule Team Borax™ and warm water, and work it into the stained area. Let this dry and brush off. Repeat as needed. You can also try pulling the fabric tight over a bowl, using a rubber band to secure it. Sprinkle Twenty Mule Team Borax™ over the stain and, using the hottest water possible for the fabric type, start at the outside edge of the stain and pour the water through the borax in circles until you are pouring through the center of the stain.

Fresh fruit stains, if treated promptly, will usually come out. Quick treatment is especially important for fruits such as peach and citrus.

Old Fruit Stains: Before you can remove the stain you must reconstitute it. You can do this by applying glycerin to the area. Rub it in well and allow to soak for 30 minutes. Treat as above.

For nonwashable fabrics, gently sponge the stain with

cold water as soon as it occurs and then take to a dry cleaner as quickly as possible. Be sure to identify the stain so it can be treated properly.

If the stains are red in nature, use Wine Away Red Wine Stain Remover™ as directed in the section on berry stains.

FURNITURE POLISH: Furniture polish is usually an oil-based stain, so it must be reconstituted. Restore the oil in the polish by spraying with WD-40 Lubricant®. Allow the lubricant to soak for 10 minutes, then work in undiluted dishwashing liquid. Work this in well between your thumbs to remove the grease. Flush with a forceful stream of the hottest water you can for the fabric type. Pretreat with a product such as Zout™, which is great for grease spots, and launder as usual.

You can also try cleaning the area with Energine Cleaning Fluid®, used according to can directions.

If the furniture polish has color in it, refer to the section on dye.

GLUE, ADHESIVES, MUCILAGE: Modern adhesives and glues are very hard to remove. You may have to use a special solvent. Take the garment to the dry cleaner and be sure to identify the spot.

Here's a rundown of glue types and how to remove them.

Model Glue: Can usually be removed with nail polish remover containing acetone, although you may need to purchase straight acetone at the hardware store or the beauty supply. Always test the acetone in a small area first.

Plastic Adhesives: For best results, treat these stains before they dry. Try washing in cool water and detergent. If the stain remains, bring 1 cup or so of white vinegar to a boil, and immerse the stain. Have more vinegar boiling as you treat the stain so that you can switch to the hot vinegar as soon as the first cup starts to cool. Continue reheating the vinegar and treating for 15 to 20 minutes.

Rubber Cement: Scrape off all that you can with a dull, straight edge that you can throw away. (Don't use a credit card for this—unless it's over its limit!) Treat with Energine Cleaning Fluid® as directed.

You can also try working petroleum jelly into the glue until it pills into balls that you can then scrape from the fabric. Treat the area with undiluted liquid dish soap and launder in the hottest water the fabric will tolerate.

Miscellaneous Glues: Sponge or rinse the fabric in warm water. Work in your favorite powdered detergent or liquid detergent along with some Twenty Mule Team Borax™. Rub vigorously between your thumbs. Rinse and wash in the hottest water you can for the fabric type.

Remember, soap and water will remove most synthetic glue when the spot is fresh. Acetone will remove most clear, plastic cement-type glues. Make sure to test acetone in an inconspicuous area, and never use on acetate fabrics—it will dissolve them.

For old, dried glue stains, soak the fabric in a solution of boiling hot white vinegar and water. Use 2 parts white vinegar to every 10 parts of water and soak for 30 to 60 minutes. You may need to scrape off the glue as it softens. Then pretreat and launder as usual.

GRASS, FLOWERS AND FOLIAGE: There are several ways to remove grass stains from fabrics. Pick one and try it. If it doesn't completely remove the stain, try another. Don't put clothes into the dryer until the grass stain is removed.

First a word of caution: Avoid using alkalis such as ammonia, degreasers or alkaline detergents. They interact with the tannin in the grass stains and may permanently set the stain.

Okay—first, washable fabrics: Sponge on rubbing alcohol, repeating several times. If the stain persists, sponge with white vinegar and rinse. Work in your favorite laundry detergent and rinse well.

Rubbing white nongel toothpaste into grass stains will often remove them. Rub well, then rinse and wash as usual.

For jeans, apply undiluted alcohol to the area and allow to soak 15 minutes before laundering as usual.

Zout™ and Spot Shot Carpet Stain Remover® also work very well on grass stains. Follow the label directions. Biz All Fabric Bleach™ made into a paste with cold water is effective in treating stubborn grass stains too.

For grass on white leather shoes, rub the grass stain with molasses and leave it on the shoe overnight. Wash the molasses off with hot soap and water, and the grass stain should be gone.

For grass on suede fabric, including shoes, rub the stain with a sponge dipped in glycerin. Then rub with a cloth dipped in undiluted white vinegar, brush the nap gently to reset, and allow to dry and brush again. Remember: test in an inconspicuous spot first.

GRAVY: With gravy you need to remove the starch used to thicken it, so you will want to soak the garment in cold water long enough to dissolve the starch. It may take several hours.

Pretreat prior to laundering with a good spotter, such as Zout™, Spot Shot Carpet Stain Remover® or Whink Wash Away Laundry Stain Remover™. Launder in the hottest possible water for the fabric type.

You can also soak the garment in Brilliant Bleach™, for days if necessary.

GREASE AND OIL (including cooking oil and salad dressing): Grease and oil must be removed thoroughly, otherwise a semitransparent stain will set and will turn dark from all the soil it attracts.

To treat a grease stain it helps to know whether it is from animal oil, vegetable oil or automotive oil.

To remove a grease stain, first remove as much of the greasy substance as possible without forcing the grease further down into the fabric fibers. Use a paper towel to blot and absorb all the grease that you can. Next, apply a drawing agent such as baking soda, cornstarch, or talcum powder. Rub it in gently and let it sit for 15 to 30 minutes to allow the agent to absorb and draw the grease out of the fabric. Brush the powder off thoroughly and check the stain. If it looks like you can absorb more grease, repeat the process.

Next, lay the fabric over a thick rag or a heavy fold of paper towels. Working from the back of the fabric, blot with Energine Cleaning Fluid®. Change the pad under the fabric as needed and repeat if necessary.

When grease stains are stubborn, we need to fall back on the idea that grease removes grease. Spray the grease spot with WD-40 Lubricant® and let it soak for 10 minutes, then work in undiluted dishwashing liquid and work well between your thumbs. Flush with the hottest water you can for the fabric, pretreat and launder as usual. Do not use this method on silk or crease-resistant finishes.

Many grease stains will eventually turn yellow when set with age and heat. Treat these stains by soaking in diluted hydrogen peroxide or Brilliant Bleach™. Don't use this process unless you know that the clothes are colorfast.

Use Energine Cleaning Fluid® on dry-clean-only fabrics, or take to a professional dry cleaner.

For heavily soiled, greasy work clothes, try pouring a can of original Coca-Cola® in the washer with your detergent and launder as usual. The combination of sugar and cola syrup works wonders!

GUM: The best way to deal with gum is to harden it first. Harden any item marred by chewing gum by placing it in a plastic bag in the freezer and leaving it overnight. Immediately upon removing the bag from the freezer, scrape off any gum that you can with a dull straight edge. If all the gum is removed, treat the fabric with an equal mixture of white vinegar and liquid dish soap. You may also try treating the area with lighter fluid, although you must do this outside and use extreme care, testing the fabric first.

Sometimes rubbing the area with egg white (*not* the yolk—no joke!) will remove the remaining residue.

If gum is still trapped, try working petroleum jelly into the fibers, and scraping off the little balls that form. Be sure to follow the directions under **Grease** in this section to remove the grease from the petroleum jelly.

Petroleum jelly will also soften old, dry gum. You want to work the petroleum jelly into the gum and then scrape off all that you can.

For those of you who ask, yes, peanut butter will work too, but it is messier. My advice is to eat the peanut butter and use the petroleum jelly!

Carbona® makes a Stain Devil for Chewing Gum Removal. It's a great little specialty spotter.

For dry-clean-only fabrics, you may freeze the fabric and scrape off what gum you can. Take it to your dry cleaner right away.

HAIR DYE: If you didn't listen to me when I told you to dye your hair naked in the backyard, then hair-dye spots may be a major problem for you. Here's what to do:

Clothing or fabrics stained with hair dye should be washed in warm water, to which you have added white vinegar and your normal detergent. Do this in a sink or container, adding about 2 tablespoons of detergent and 2 cups of white vinegar to a gallon of warm water. Let it soak for several hours.

If the stain still remains, try our favorite bleach, Brilliant Bleach™. You can soak whites and colorfast fabrics for several days if necessary, without damage. Try to avoid the hair dye problem if you can. I suggest using the same old towel when you do your hair.

HAND CREAM: Blot off all that you can and treat with Energine Cleaning Fluid®, working from the back of the fabric. Once all of the stain is removed, launder as usual.

ICE CREAM: Yummy-yummy in the tummy—not so great on clothes! Sponge the garment as quickly as possible with cold water, club soda, or seltzer. If a stain still remains, treat it with cold water and unseasoned meat tenderizer. Let this soak on the fabric for about 30 minutes or so and then flush with cold water to see if the offending spot is gone. Pretreat with Spot Shot Carpet Stain Remover® or Zout™ and launder as usual.

If a grease spot remains, treat with Energine Cleaning Fluid® working from the back of the fabric over a pad of paper towels to absorb the spot and the spotting solution.

Sometimes treating ice cream–stained fabric with a small amount of ammonia will also work. Then, of course, launder as usual.

INK: How can one little pen cause so much grief? The first line of offense is rubbing alcohol. Sponge the ink mark, or dip it into a glass of rubbing alcohol, letting it soak until the offending spot is removed. Don't be tricked into using hair spray. That may have worked in the past, but hair spray now contains a lot of oil, and that just spreads the stain.

Denatured alcohol—a much stronger version of rubbing alcohol—may be more effective. Test this first in an inconspicuous spot, as denatured alcohol may damage some fabrics. You also can try using acetone. This too must be tested. (And remember, *never* use acetone on acetates.)

White, nongel toothpaste rubbed firmly and vigorously into the stain may work. After this method be sure to pretreat and launder as usual.

Often just soaking ink stains in milk will dissolve them.

Turpentine is effective on very challenging ink stains. Working over a pad of paper towels, tap the spot on the back of the fabric using the back of a spoon or an old toothbrush. Don't rub. Work in undiluted dishwashing liquid prior to laundering, and wash in the hottest water possible for the fabric type. Dispose of all paper, etc., saturated with turpentine immediately—outside, please.

Some inks only respond to solvents, so you may need to use Energine Cleaning Fluid®.

On leather, remove ballpoint ink by rubbing with cuticle remover or petroleum jelly. You may need to leave it on the stained area for several days to achieve success.

On vinyl, believe it or not, the best thing is for you to be so mad that you could spit! Saliva will remove ballpoint ink from vinyl—as long as you are quick. Apply generously and wipe with a soft cloth. For old stains, apply glycerin, let it soak for 30 minutes or so, and then attempt to wash the stain away with a wet soft cloth rubbed over a bar of soap.

KETCHUP: See *Tomato-Based Stains.*

KOOL-AID™: Flush the spot as quickly as possible with club soda and then hold under forceful running water. If a stained area still remains, soak in Brilliant Bleach™ until the stain is removed. This may take hours or days, depending on the fabric and the stain. Soak only white or colorfast clothes in Brilliant Bleach™.

For red, grape, fruit punch, and other red Kool-Aid™ flavors, treat with Wine Away Red Wine Stain Remover™ for instantaneous stain removal.

LIPSTICK: Lipstick is actually an oily dye stain. Water, heat or wet spotters will only spread it and make the problem worse and set the stain.

Rub in vegetable oil, WD-40 Lubricant® or mineral oil and let it sit on the spot for 15 to 30 minutes. Next sponge the area with a little ammonia—sudsy or clear is fine.

Now, before you launder, work in undiluted liquid dish soap to be sure you have removed all of the oil.

Another method I have had real success with is Go-Jo Creme Waterless Hand Cleaner™. Look for this at hardware stores and home centers. Work it into the lipstick, rubbing between your thumbs vigorously. Launder as usual. This method is great for the smear of lipstick on cloth table napkins.

In an emergency, try spraying the spot with a little hair spray. Let this sit for a few minutes and then wipe gently with a damp cloth. Test this method in an inconspicuous spot first.

You will also find that Zout™, Spot Shot Carpet Stain Remover® and Whink Wash Away Laundry Spotter™ are generally effective on lipstick.

For really stubborn, old stains, try moistening with denatured alcohol, then treat with undiluted liquid dish soap.

If you are getting dressed and you accidentally get lipstick on your clothes, try rubbing the stain with white bread. (Yes, it has to be white!)

MAKEUP (oily foundation, powder, cream blush, cover creams):
Sprinkle baking soda on the makeup smudge, then brush the area with an old wet toothbrush until the makeup is removed. Nongel white toothpaste scrubbed with a toothbrush is also effective.

Liquid dish soap or shampoo will generally remove makeup stains. Work the product into the stain vigorously between your thumbs.

For stubborn makeup stains use nonoily makeup remover, pretreat and launder as usual. (See also **Cosmetics.**)

MARKER, WASHABLE: Rinse the stain from the fabric with cold water until no more color can be removed. Place the fabric on paper towels and saturate the back of the fabric with alcohol, using a cotton ball to blot the stain. Replace the paper towels as needed as they absorb the color. Work in Fels-Naptha Soap® until the spot is well lathered and wash in hot water with laundry detergent and fabric appropriate bleach. Rinse in warm water.

MARKER, PERMANENT: First of all, permanent usually means permanent. But before you give up and throw in the towel— or blouse, or pants, or whatever—here are some things to try.

Fill a glass with denatured alcohol (use a size appropriate to the stain) and dip the stained area into the alcohol, allowing it to soak. If it appears that the marker is being removed, continue the process.

If the stain appears stubborn, try scrubbing the marker spot with an old toothbrush, white, nongel toothpaste, and some baking soda. Give it a really good scrubbing. Rinse. If the marker stain is almost gone, soak in a cup of warm water and 2 denture-cleaning tablets for whites, and Brilliant Bleach™ for colorfast clothes. This will require some time, but the stain all comes out, so it's worth it.

If the marker is still there, scrub with Lava™ soap prior to trying the denture-cleaning tablets or bleach.

Good luck. And look out for those big black permanent markers and those Sharpies™. They're great pens, but they're murder on clothes! I can't even tell you how many times I have "accidentally" written on my clothes during a book signing with a Sharpie™ in my hand!

MAYONNAISE: See *Grease*.

MEAT JUICES: Once dry, meat juices are very tough to remove, so it's important to react quickly. Sponge the area immediately with cold water (not hot—it will set the stain), or with club soda. Next, apply unseasoned meat tenderizer and cold water, working the mixture in well. Let it sit for 30 to 60 minutes. Pretreat and launder as usual, but be sure to use *cool* water.

On dry-clean-only fabrics, sponge with cold water and take to a professional cleaner.

MEDICINES: It would be impossible to list all the medicines on the market. But this section should give you an idea of what to look out for, as well as what to do for each family of medicine.

Alcohol: Medicines containing alcohol stain quickly. Treat these stains as you would spilled alcohol.

Iron: Iron or medicines containing iron products should be treated as rust.

Oily Medicines: Oily medicines should be treated with a degreasing product. I have had great luck with Soapworks At Home All-Purpose Cleaner™, used undiluted. Work it in well and then rinse.

You can also treat these stains as you would an oil or grease stain.

Syrups: Cough syrup or children's medicines can usually be removed with water. Soak the fabric with cool water as soon as possible. Running cold water full force through the fabric can be helpful, and you may also want to try working in Fels-Naptha®, or soaking the stain in Biz Non Chlorine Bleach™ or Brilliant Bleach™. If the syrup is red, use Wine Away Red Wine Stain Remover™. (See, I told you not to be fooled by its name! It is murder on red stains!)

MILDEW: Mildew is a fungus that grows and flourishes in warm, humid, dark conditions, like the shower, the basement, etc. The best way to avoid mildew is to ensure that things are totally dry *before* you put them away. Invisible spores can quickly grow to huge proportions, especially on natural materials such as cotton, wool, leather, paper, wood, etc.

Air needs to circulate to keep mildew from forming, so do not crowd clothes into closets.

Store clothing only after it has been cleaned and dried thoroughly.

If you are storing things such as leather purses, belts, shoes, even suitcases, clean them well, then sit them in the sun for an hour or so. Do not store things in plastic as this caters to damp conditions.

If you smell a damp or musty smell coming from a closet, suspect mildew immediately and act quickly to dry it out. Even allowing a fan to blow in the closet overnight can make a huge difference by drying and circulating the air.

Okay—here's what to do if you already have mildew stains on fabrics. First, try working some Fels-Naptha Laundry Bar Soap® into the area and laundering. If stains remain and the fabric will tolerate chlorine bleach, soak it in 1 gallon of cold water to which you have added 2 to 3 table-spoons of chlorine bleach.

Moistening white or colorfast clothes with lemon juice, sprinkling them with salt and laying the garment in the sun may also remove mildew. If in doubt, test this method first.

Leather presents a different challenge. Take the item outside and brush off all the powdery mildew that you can with a soft brush. Wipe the leather with equal parts of rubbing alcohol and water, or try massaging cuticle remover into the area. After 10 minutes, wipe vigorously with a soft cloth.

Wash leather with a complexion bar soap such as Dove® or Caress™ and buff dry—do not rinse.

Remember: with mildew, the best defense is a good offense, so try to keep it from occurring.

MILK/CREAM/WHIPPING CREAM/HALF AND HALF: Rinse fabric under a cold, forceful stream of water from the faucet. Treat with unseasoned meat tenderizer and cool water. Allow to soak for 30 minutes, then flush with cool water again. If greasy-looking marks remain, treat with Energine Cleaning Fluid®, working from the back of the fabric over a heavy pad of paper towels. Launder as usual.

Treat washable fabrics stained from milk by flushing with cool water before working in detergent and a little ammonia. Wash in cool water and air-dry.

For dry-clean-only fabrics, take to a professional as soon as possible and identify the stain when you drop off the item.

MUD: The key word here is *dry*. Let mud dry. Never treat a wet mud stain other than lifting off any solid pieces with a dull straight edge. Once mud has dried, take the vacuum cleaner and vacuum the area with the hose attachment. You'll achieve the greatest suction that way. This may be a two-person job. One to hold the fabric, one to hold the hose. Rub the cut side of a potato over the mud stain and launder as usual.

For stubborn stains, sponge with equal portions of rubbing alcohol and cool water. For red mud stains, treat with a rust remover. (See *Rust*). Rubbing Twenty Mule Team Borax™ into a dampened mud stain will often remove it.

Spraying with Spot Shot Carpet Stain Remover® prior to laundering is also helpful.

MUSTARD: The word makes me shiver! This is a terrible stain to attempt (notice I said *attempt*) to remove.

The turmeric in mustard is what gives mustard its distinctive bright yellow color—it's also what would make it a darn good dye!

Remove as much of the mustard as possible, using a dull straight edge. Next, flex the fabric to break the grip of the embedded residue on the fabric fibers. Apply glycerin (hand cream section, drugstore) and let it sit at least an hour. Pretreat and launder as usual.

If the fabric is white or colorfast, soak the stain in hydrogen peroxide for 30 minutes. Again, Brilliant Bleach™ may remove the stain after a lengthy soaking.

For white clothes, dissolve a denture-cleaning tablet in ½ cup of cool water and allow the stained area to soak.

Things to avoid: Ammonia and heat. They will both set the stain and you will never get it out.

Kind of makes you think that ketchup and relish are all you need on that hotdog, doesn't it!

MYSTERY STAINS: These are spots and spills that you have no idea where they came from. The unknowns. Here's what to do:

- Blot with cool water (hot water sets stains).

- Blot with a sponge or cloth dampened with water and a teaspoon or so of white vinegar (not for cotton or linen).

- Blot with a sponge or cloth dampened with water and a teaspoon or so of clear ammonia (again, not for cotton or linen).

- Blot with rubbing alcohol diluted 50/50 with cool water.

- Sponge with a solution of Brilliant Bleach™ and water.

NAIL POLISH: Okay, if you had polished your nails naked in the backyard you wouldn't be reading this, would you? Stretch the fabric over a glass bowl and make a little trampoline by securing the fabric with a rubber band. Drip acetone-based polish remover through the stain with a stainless steel spoon (not silver) and tap the stain with the edge of the spoon. Continue dripping the acetone through the fabric until the polish is removed. This requires time and patience. If you run out of either, walk away and come back later. Straight acetone, purchased at the hardware store or beauty supply, may work faster, but be sure to test an area first.

If a color stain remains after the polish is removed, dilute hydrogen peroxide (50 percent peroxide, 50 percent water) apply to the stain, and sit the fabric in the sun, keeping it moist with the peroxide solution. Do this only for white or colorfast clothes.

Do not use acetone on silk or acetates, and always test the acetone on an inconspicuous area prior to beginning.

Nonwashable fabrics should be dry-cleaned.

ODORS: Eliminate odors, don't use a perfumed cover-up. I like ODORZOUT™ odor eliminator because it absorbs odors and removes them permanently—without leaving any telltale smells behind. It is nontoxic and safe for all surfaces, and it can be used wet or dry. It is also safe for the environment and a little goes a long way. Keep some on hand. It's great for just about any odor you're likely to come across, such as smoke, mildew, mold, feces, urine, food odors, any kind of odor. Do not use a perfumed cover-up.

OIL (also see **Grease and Oil):** Blot up all oil quickly. Avoid rubbing or you will force the oil further into the fibers. Pretreat washable fabrics with your favorite spot remover, or use one recommended for oily stains in this book. Launder in the hottest possible water for the fabric.

Nonwashables should be dry-cleaned.

OINTMENT (A and D ointment, Desitin, zinc oxide): Anyone who has had a baby will be familiar with this problem stain. Use hot water and detergent, rubbing the fabric against itself to remove the oil. If the stain remains, treat as indicated in the section on **Grease and Oil.**

For zinc oxide, soak the garment in white vinegar for 30 minutes after treating as above, then launder as usual.

PAINT, LATEX: Treat this stain immediately for best results. It is important to remove paint *before* it dries, so keep the stain wet if you can't work on it right away.

Flush the paint from the fabric with a forceful stream of warm water. Next, treat the stain with a solution of liquid dish soap and water, or laundry detergent and water. Work it into the stained area, soaping and rinsing until the stain is removed. Do this as many times as necessary. If the fabric is colorfast, you can also work in some automatic dishwasher detergent and let it soak on the fabric for 5 to 10 minutes before laundering as usual.

You can also try a product aptly named OOPS!™ Just follow the directions on the can closely.

On fabrics such as cotton and polyester, try spraying the garment with oven cleaner and letting it sit about 15 to 30 minutes before flushing with plenty of water. Use *extreme* care with this method and use it at your own risk. Some fabrics cannot tolerate the oven cleaner, but if the garment is ruined by the paint, it is worth a try. Also use care where you spray the oven cleaner and what you sit the fabric on afterward.

PAINT, OIL-BASED: Get busy and remove this spill ASAP. You're out of luck if it dries. If you must go to the store for products, keep the spill moist: *Do not allow oil-based paint to dry.*

Check the paint can and use the thinner recommended by the manufacturer. Sometimes thinner for correction fluid will also work. Remember to test an area first with these two methods.

I fall back on turpentine when all else fails. Work the turpentine into the spill, and once the paint is removed, work in Go-Jo Creme Waterless Hand Cleaner™. That will take out the oiliness from the turpentine. Remember to dispose of turpentine soaked rags or paper towels outside, as soon as possible.

When working on a paint spill, work from the back of the fabric over a thick pad of paper towels. Tap the stained area with an old toothbrush or an old spoon as you work to force the paint out.

Now that you have removed the stain, saturate it with detergent and work in vigorously. Cover the area with the hottest water you can use for the fabric, and let it soak overnight. Scrub again, between your thumbs, and launder as usual.

PENCIL: Okay, how easy is this? Take a nice, clean, soft eraser, and gently rub the offending mark away! Just be sure the eraser is clean, or you will create a large stain. If the spot is stubborn, sponge with Energine Cleaning Fluid®.

PERFUME: Follow the directions in the section on *Alcoholic Beverages.* A few words to the wise: The best time to put it on is right before you put on your clothes, not after. And never spray perfume directly on your clothes. This will damage them. The combination of alcohol and oil is death to fabrics.

PERSPIRATION STAINS: These stains really are the pits, so I've devoted an entire chapter to their removal. Also check out the section in this stain removal guide on *Antiperspirants and Deodorants.*

PURPLE OR BLUISH COLOR ON SYNTHETIC FIBERS: Sometimes synthetic fibers will develop a purple tinge after repeated laundering. Remove it with Rit Color Remover™ and launder as usual.

RUST: On white fabrics, saturate with lemon juice and sprinkle with salt, then lay in the sun. (No, not you—the fabric!) If the rust is stubborn, apply the lemon juice and salt, and pour water through the stain. Use boiling water if the fabric will tolerate it; otherwise use hot. Check the care label.

You can also cover the stained area with cream of tartar, then gather up the edges of the fabric and dip the spot in hot water. Let stand 5 to 10 minutes and then launder as usual.

There are good commercial rust removers on the market. Try Whink Rust Remover®, Magica®, and Rust Magic®. Be sure to read directions carefully when using commercial rust removers. Some cannot be used on colored fabric, so check carefully.

SAP, PINE TAR: See *Tar.*

SCORCH MARKS: Sorry to say, but severe scorch marks cannot be removed.

Light scorch marks may be treated with a cloth dampened with 1 part 3 percent hydrogen peroxide and 3 parts of water. Lay the cloth over the scorch mark and press with a medium/hot iron. Do not iron off of the cloth or you will scorch the fabric again. Make sure to try this method first in a small, inconspicuous space.

If the scorch is still visible, moisten the spot with the diluted peroxide and lay it in the sun.

Very light scorch marks may also be removed by wetting them with water and laying the garment in the sun.

If the scorch mark has appeared on white clothes, saturate the scorched area with lemon juice and lay it in the sun. Keep it moist with the lemon juice until the stain is removed.

For white cottons, sometimes boiling in ½ cup of soap and 2 quarts of milk will remove the stain. Try this at your own risk. Some fabrics may not tolerate boiling.

For light scorches you can also rub the fabric with the cut side of a white onion (not a red onion—it will stain) and then soak the fabric in cold water for several hours. Launder as usual.

Remember: scorching weakens fibers, so use care and always relaunder the item once the scorch mark has been removed.

SHOE POLISH: Work laundry detergent into the fabric immediately and rinse. For persistent stains, sponge with alcohol. Use undiluted alcohol on white clothes, and 1 part alcohol to 2 parts water on colored fabrics. Rinse again, or try using turpentine after first testing in an inconspicuous spot.

Shoe polish has an oily base containing dye. Using the

wrong things such as water, heat, or wet spotters will spread and set the stain. Work in vegetable oil or WD-40 Lubricant® and let it sit for 15 minutes. Sponge on a little ammonia (not on silk, please), then work in undiluted dishwashing liquid and launder as usual.

Energine Cleaning Fluid® may also help to eliminate the final stained area.

If you have any discoloration remaining from the dye in the shoe polish, soak the fabric in Brilliant Bleach™ until the stain is removed.

If the shoe polish stain is old and heavy, you may need to treat it with petroleum jelly. Cover the polish and work in the petroleum jelly, let it soak for 30 to 60 minutes, and then scrape off all that you can of the polish and the petroleum jelly. Work in undiluted dishwashing liquid and flush with a forceful stream of hot water. Pretreat and launder as usual.

Liquid Shoe Polish: Blot up all that you can from the fabric. Do not rub—this will spread the stain. Do not apply water. Instead, saturate with alcohol—undiluted for whites, diluted as above for colors. Continue to flush with alcohol, work in your favorite laundry detergent, then rub vigorously to remove all trace of the stain.

SILK SPOTS: Spots on silk are hard to remove and must be handled with care.

Dry-cleaning solvent may spot-clean silk, but you're likely to be left with a ring on the fabric. Make sure to use the blow-dryer on the spot to avoid that telltale ring.

For unusual or heavy stains, take to a professional. Too much rubbing can remove the color from silk.

SILLY PUTTY®: First of all, let gravity do the work for you.

Lay the fabric over a bowl and let it simply drop off. You'll only have to clean up what's left!

Scrape off the balance of any Silly Putty® with a dull edge such as an old credit card or knife back. Spray with WD-40 Lubricant® and let stand a few minutes. Scrape again, removing all the Silly Putty® that you can. Continue to do this, changing from the dull straight edge to cotton balls. If any stain remains, saturate a cotton ball with rubbing alcohol, blot the stain, and rinse. Work in liquid dish soap and launder as usual in the hottest water you can for the fabric type.

If you don't have WD-40 Lubricant®, use petroleum jelly instead.

SOFT DRINKS: See *Colas and Soft Drinks.*

SOOT: Launder clothing in the hottest possible water for the fabric with your normal detergent, ½ cup of Twenty Mule Team Borax™ and ½ cup of Arm and Hammer Washing Soda™.

STICKERS: Heat white vinegar and apply it, undiluted, directly to the fabric. Allow the vinegar to soak until the sticker can be peeled back with ease.

TAR: Lift off as much solid matter as possible using a plastic (disposable) knife. Spread the stained area over a heavy pad of paper towels and apply glycerin to the fabric, tapping it with the back of an old toothbrush or plastic spoon. Change the paper towels as they absorb the tar. Finally, once you have removed all the tar you can, work in some turpentine or eucalyptus oil. Flush the stained area with alcohol, or work in undiluted liquid dish soap. Pretreat and launder as usual. Spot Shot Carpet Stain Remover® is a good spotter for this.

Dried Tar: Warm the glycerin or some olive oil and spread

over the area, allowing it to soak until the tar is loosened. Then proceed as above.

Nonwashables should be taken to the dry cleaner as soon as possible.

TEA: See *Coffee and Tea.*

TOMATO-BASED STAINS (ketchup, spaghetti sauce, tomato sauce, barbecue sauce, etc.): Flush these stains well with cool water as soon as possible. Make sure you apply water to the back of the fabric. Apply white vinegar and then flush again with a forceful stream of water.

Apply Wine Away Red Wine Stain Remover™ per package directions.

URINE: Fresh urine stains are fairly easy to remove. First rinse well, flushing with lots of cool water. Presoak using an enzyme powder or Biz All Fabric Bleach™. Then launder as usual.

You may also soak urine-stained fabric in salt water, then rinse and launder as usual.

If the color of the fabric has changed due to the urine, sponge the area or spray with clear ammonia, then rinse and launder as usual.

For Old Urine Stains: Soak in clear hot water for an hour—the hotter the better. Add detergent and wash as usual, then rinse. Use the appropriate bleach for the fabric type, or Brilliant Bleach™ if you prefer.

See also the treatment mentioned under *Odors.*

VOMIT: Shake off or scrape what you can over the toilet. Flush the fabric from the wrong side with cool water, using a forceful stream. Once you have removed solid matter and excess liquid, make a paste of liquid laundry soap and Twenty-Mule

Team Borax™ and vigorously scrub the fabric. Rinse with salt water, pretreat and launder as usual.

Quick treatment is important to avoid stains from foods and stomach acid.

See also the treatment mentioned for **Odors.**

WINE: Never serve red wine without having white wine nearby! And always tend to the stain *as soon as you can!*

For red wine spills, dilute the spot with white wine, then flush with cool water and apply salt.

If no white wine is available, sprinkle heavily with salt and flush with club soda or cool water.

Applying a paste of Twenty Mule Team Borax™ and water usually works.

For red wine spills and other red stains, keep Wine Away Red Wine Stain Remover™ on hand. It is totally nontoxic and works so fast on red wine and red stains that even I am still amazed. The directions are simple and easy. Blot up the spill, apply the Wine Away™ and watch the red stain disappear. Blot with a wet cloth. You'll thank me many times for this one!

YELLOW SPOTS AND STAINS: These stains are common on white clothes and linens. Denture-cleaning tablets will generally remove these stains. Fill a basin with water and add one or two tablets. Allow the tablets to dissolve and then soak the fabric until the yellow is removed.

Resource Guide

ACETONE: A great spotter, but be careful. It is exceedingly strong and can damage fibers. Look for this at hardware stores, home centers and beauty supply stores.

ACT NATURAL CLOTHS®: See Euronet USA.

BIZ® ACTIVATED NON CHLORINE BLEACH: A great all-purpose powdered bleach. Look for it in the laundry aisle at grocery stores and discount stores.

BORAX: Better known as Twenty Mule Team Borax® Laundry Additive. This can be found in the detergent aisle.

BRILLIANT BLEACH™: See Soapworks.

CARBONA® COLOR RUN REMOVER: Removes fugitive color from fabrics. Available in grocery and discount stores.

CARBONA® STAIN DEVILS: A great series of spotters that target specific stains, like gum, blood, milk, etc.

CLEAR AMMONIA: There are two types of ammonia, clear and sudsy (sometimes called "cloudy"). Clear doesn't contain soap and should be used where suggested for that reason.

CLEAN SHIELD® SURFACE TREATMENT (formerly Invisible Shield®):
This is such a wonderful product—just the name gives me goose bumps! It turns all of those hard-to-clean surfaces in your home (the exterior of the washing machine and dryer, any surface that is not wood or painted) into nonstick surfaces that can be cleaned with water and a soft cloth. No more soap scum or hard-water deposits! It never builds up so it won't make surfaces slipperier, and it's nontoxic too! Call 1-800-528-3149 for a supplier near you.

CUSTOM CLEANER®: Try this if you're looking for a do-it-yourself dry-cleaning kit to freshen and spot-clean clothes. I love it. Custom Cleaner® works on all kinds of spots and has a very pleasant, clean scent. Look for this at grocery stores and discount stores.

DENATURED ALCOHOL: This is an industrial alcohol reserved for heavy-duty cleaning. Don't use it near an open flame, and make sure to dispose outside the home any rags that were used to apply it. Launder or clean anything that you treat with it as soon as possible. Look for this in cans at hardware stores and home centers.

DE-SOLV-IT CITRUS SOLUTION™: Available in home centers, hardware stores, etc., De-Solv-It Citrus-Solution™ has a multitude of uses both inside and out. Great for laundry.

ENERGINE CLEANING FLUID®: A great spotter. Look for this at the hardware store, the home center, and even in some grocery stores (usually on the top shelf with the laundry additives).

EPSOM SALTS: Usually used for medicinal purposes, but handy for laundry too. Look for this in the drugstore.

EURONET USA: Makers of Act Natural® microfiber cloths. These easy-to-use cloths have been scientifically proven to kill germs and bacteria. They even come with a warranty. I never travel without a cloth, and I keep one in my desk and briefcase to quickly clean up any of those little spills on clothes. Call 1-888-638-2882 or visit www.euronetusa.com

FELS-NAPTHA HEAVY-DUTY LAUNDRY BAR SOAP®: You'll find this wonderful laundry spotter and cleaner in the bar soap section of the grocery store. It's usually on the bottom shelf covered in dust, because nobody knows what to use it for!

FRESH BREEZE LAUNDRY SOAP®: See Soapworks.

GLYCERIN: Look for glycerin in drugstores in the hand cream section. Always purchase plain glycerin, *not* the type containing rosewater.

GO-JO WATERLESS HAND CLEANER®: Not just a hand cleaner, Go-Jo is great for laundry too. Look for it at home centers and hardware stores.

HYDROGEN PEROXIDE: Make sure to choose 3 percent—the type used for cuts, *not* the type used to bleach hair. (That's too strong and will remove color from fabric.)

MEAT TENDERIZER: Great for spotting protein stains. Use the unseasoned variety please, or you will have a whole new stain to deal with. Store brands work fine.

NAIL POLISH REMOVER: I caution you to use nonacetone polish remover first. It's much less aggressive than acetone polish remover.

NONGEL TOOTHPASTE: This is just a fancy name for old-fashioned plain white toothpaste. Gels just don't work, so don't even try.

ODORZOUT®: A fabulous, dry, 100 percent natural deodorizer. It's nontoxic, so you can use it anyplace you have a smell or a stink. Also available in a pouch for shoes, laundry hampers, etc. Call 1-800-88STINK, or visit their website at www.88stink.com

PUREX® LAUNDRY DETERGENT: Available wherever detergents are sold.

RETAYNE®: Used *before* you launder colored clothes for the first time, it will help retain color. Available wherever quilting supplies are sold.

RUST REMOVER: These are serious products, so follow the directions carefully. Look for products like Whink® and Rust Magic® at hardware stores and home centers.

SHAVING CREAM: The cheaper brands work fine for spotting. Cream works better than gel.

SOAPWORKS: Manufacturer of wonderful nontoxic, user-friendly and earth-friendly cleaning, laundry, and personal care products. Try their Fresh Breeze Laundry Powder®, originally designed for allergy and asthma sufferers. Also try their Brilliant Bleach®. Believe me, it *is* brilliant! Call 1-800-699-9917 or visit their website at www.soapworks.com

SOOT AND DIRT REMOVAL SPONGE: These big brick erasers are available at home centers and hardware stores, usually near the wallpaper supplies. Clean them by washing in a pail of warm water and liquid dish soap, rinse well, and allow to dry before using again.

SPOT SHOT INSTANT CARPET STAIN REMOVER®: My all-time favorite carpet spotter is a wonderful laundry spotter too! Available most everywhere, or call 1-800-848-4389.

SYNTHRAPOL®: Great for removing fugitive color. Available wherever quilting supplies are sold.

UN-DU™: Removes sticky residue from fabric and hard surfaces. Look for it at office supply, home centers and hardware stores.

WASHING SODA: I like Arm and Hammer® Washing Soda, which can be found in the detergent aisle at the grocery store along with other laundry additives. No, you cannot substitute baking soda; it's a different product!

WD-40® LUBRICANT: Fine spray oil for lubricating all kinds of things, WD-40® is wonderful for regenerating grease so that it can be removed from clothes. Look for this at the hardware store, home center, and even the grocery store.

WIEMAN'S WAX AWAY™: Removes candle wax from fabrics and hard surfaces. Look for it at grocery stores and discount stores.

WINE AWAY RED WINE STAIN REMOVER™: This unbelievably good product can be found at Linens 'n Things, or wherever liquor is sold. Call 1-888-WINEAWAY for a store near you.

ZOUT STAIN REMOVER®: A very versatile laundry pre-spotter, Zout® is thicker than most laundry spotters, so you can target the spot. It really works! Buy it in grocery stores, discount stores, etc.

Index

AN EXCERPT FROM

A Queen for All Seasons

A Year of Tips, Tricks, and Picks
for a Cleaner House
and a More Organized Life!

LINDA COBB

NOW AVAILABLE FROM
POCKET BOOKS

 March

It's spring! The flowers are blooming, the birds are singing, everything's fresh and new, and you can't wait to get started with your spring-cleaning. Yikes! Did I say spring-cleaning? That has no part in my spring fantasy. How about yours? Spring-cleaning was a necessity a long time ago when log cabins were boarded up to keep out the winter cold. The arrival of spring presented the first opportunity to clean out all the soot and grime that had accumulated during the long winter months—hence the term spring-cleaning. Those of you living in log cabins may want to continue this practice, but for the rest of us, well, there are better things to do.

That's not to say that there aren't certain times of the year when you'll want to clean a little more thoroughly. It may be just after Christmas, it may be right before Aunt Martha's next visit . . . it might even be spring. *When* you do it is entirely up to you. As for *what* to do, read on.

FIRST THINGS FIRST

Decide on your approach and be consistent. If you decide to clean for an hour, stick to it. If you decide to clean one room now and another tomorrow, stick to that. Indecision and distraction can really affect how well you clean. If you start out doing one thing and end up doing another, you'll have a houseful of half-finished projects, and you won't feel as if you've accomplished anything. That can be very frustrating, to say the least.

I like to start with the room that requires the least amount of effort, and that's generally the one that's used the least. It may be the guest room, the living room . . . it may even be the kitchen. Hey—no judgments. Think of it as a sort of warm-up. Start with the lightest task and you'll see results fast. That will motivate you to keep going!

Generally speaking, work from top to bottom. Dust from the light fixtures, tops of furniture, etc., will fall onto the carpet and floors. So do floors last and you'll know that your house really is clean.

Remember: If it isn't dirty, don't clean it!

Don't backtrack. Finish one task before moving to another. Put on some high-spirited music to set the pace and keep you going.

LET'S GET STARTED

Dusting comes first. But don't just pick up any old cloth, and don't, for heaven's sake, use a feather duster. They may be some man's fantasy, but they just scatter the dust all around. Really, they're worse than useless. I strongly recommend washable lambs wool dusters. Lambs wool both attracts and contains dust, so it won't whisk the dust around from one surface to the other. Lambs wool is also washable, so it lasts for years. (You can buy lambs wool dusters in many varieties, including dust mitts and telescoping dusters, which are great for those hard-to-reach corners.)

Use a telescoping lambs wool duster to clean ceiling fans.

Don't just move ornaments while you're dusting. Make sure to dust them, too!

After you've dusted your electronic equipment, it's a good idea to give it a wipe with some rubbing alcohol. Apply with a clean, soft cloth, then buff dry. Make sure to turn the power off first, though.

Once you've dusted, give the upholstery a good going-over. Use the appropriate attachment on your vacuum cleaner—the small brush for cushions and arms, the long nozzle for crevices and hard-to-reach areas. If you own a sofa bed, make sure to open it up and vacuum the mattress. (Most sofa bed mattresses are one-side only, so don't try to flip it.) Don't forget to vacuum scatter cushions.

Climb the walls, I mean *clean* the walls, by tying a towel over the head of a broom and pulling it down the wall. Shake out the towel as necessary, and change it when it becomes soiled. Work up and down the wall—not side to side—and use strokes that are comfortable for you. Complete one room at a time.

Walls don't need to be washed every year unless you're a smoker. So don't wash walls that don't need it. If, however, a room looks grimy, a good wall wash could save you the effort of painting.

FLOORS

Grit can scratch wood floors, so they should be swept before washing. Use long, directed strokes, moving from the corners to the center of the room. Sweep all the grit—that means crumbs, cat litter, and all that unidentifiable stuff—into a dustpan.

Now you're ready to wash with your favorite, gentle floor cleaner. Don't have a favorite wood floor cleaner? Try tea! The tannic acid gives the floor a wonderful shine. Use several tea bags to brew a quart or two. You can have a cup if you like, but let the rest cool to room temperature before using. Wring a soft cloth out in the tea. Make sure the cloth is damp, not wet. Overwetting the floor could warp it or damage the finish. Just in case I haven't been clear on this: *Yes, I am suggesting that you get down on your hands and knees.* Sorry, but anything else is just a shortcut, and if you want to clean your floors thoroughly, this is the only way to go.

- Start at the edges and move your hand across the floor, using a small circular motion.

- Keep the cloth well rinsed and continue until the entire floor is done.

- For vinyl or tile floors use the same cleaning method, substituting 1 gallon of warm water combined with 2 table-spoons of 20 Mule Team® Borax for the tea.

- For marble floors try the ACT Natural™ Microfiber

Mop. It uses nothing but water and thousands of little scrubbing fingers that pick up the dirt without scratching. It won't leave a film, either.

AND DON'T FORGET ...

• Give the inside of kitchen cupboards a wash with a simple solution of warm, soapy water. Anything sticky can be removed with a little baking soda.

• Grind some lemon rinds and ice cubes in the disposal to keep it clean and sharpen the blades, too.

• Vacuum your mattress with the upholstery attachment, then flip it for even wear. A plastic bag, such as a dry cleaner's bag, placed between the box spring and mattress will help ease the strain of this task. (Best not to take any chances, so if you have young children leave out the bag and let your muscles do the work.)

• Since you're flipping your mattress, don't forget to wash your mattress pad, blankets and pillows before putting the bed back together.

• Yes, even that self-cleaning oven needs to be cleaned.

• Draperies should be cleaned once a year. Please read the care label carefully and don't try to wash curtains that should be dry-cleaned.

You can extend the life of your window coverings by vacuuming them frequently.

- Not every room requires the same effort or attention, so decide before you begin what clean means to you.

- If you use the space under your bed for storage, remove the storage containers, vacuum the carpet and clean the containers before you put them back.

- If the woodwork on your walls is dirty, you should carefully wash it even though you do not wash the walls.

- Take down the globes from the overhead light fixtures, wash them and put them back up. While you're at it, when the lightbulbs are cool, dust them, too.

- If hinges are squeaking every time you open a door, lubricate them with a quick spray of silicone.

- Don't overlook door handles—wash and polish them. They get used constantly and seldom get washed.

Your Personal Tips and Hints

Your Personal Tips and Hints

Your Personal Tips and Hints

Your Personal Tips and Hints

ABOUT THE QUEEN

LINDA COBB first shared her cleaning tips with readers in a weekly newspaper column in Michigan, where she owned a cleaning and disaster-restoration business dealing with the aftermath of fires and floods. After moving to Phoenix, she appeared weekly as a guest on *Good Morning Arizona;* since then she has shared her housekeeping advice on radio and television shows across the country, and compiled hundreds of helpful tips in her #1 *New York Times* bestseller, *Talking Dirty with the Queen of Clean*®. Linda Cobb lives in Phoenix with her husband. Visit her popular Web site: www.queenofclean.com.